nation alone can bring the world to a golden age of peace; it begins with the individual and proceeds by faith until *all* nations demand of their leaders serenity of life, regardless of political idealogy.

This volume is indeed the voice of Man perpetuating his ancient plea for peace on earth: "So clearly do we see the need for eliminating war that we must parallel this effort with a determination to do all that lies within our power to bring all others to a realization that resort to force cannot possibly result in anything except destruction. . . ."

To those who are hostile to free government and to the religious faith upon which free government is built, these addresses are the firm reply that man has individual rights and an obligation to avoid infringement upon the equal rights of others.

To all who wish to add to their understanding of America's position in international relations, and who wish to better acquaint themselves with the objectives and ideals of our government in working for a universal peace, this book is most sincerely recommended.

PEACE WITH JUSTICE

PEACE
WITH
JUSTICE

SELECTED ADDRESSES OF

DWIGHT D. EISENHOWER

WITH A FOREWORD BY

GRAYSON KIRK

COLUMBIA UNIVERSITY PRESS

NEW YORK 1961

PUBLISHED IN GREAT BRITAIN, INDIA, AND PAKISTAN
BY THE OXFORD UNIVERSITY PRESS
LONDON, BOMBAY, AND KARACHI

LIBRARY OF CONGRESS CATALOG CARD NUMBER: 61-7096

MANUFACTURED IN THE UNITED STATES OF AMERICA

FOREWORD

Ten momentous years in the history of our country are encompassed within the span of these thirty speeches. They were years of trial brought on and sustained by the relentless outward thrusting of Soviet expansionist policy. For our country, they were years of growing maturity as we put aside, gradually and reluctantly, the cherished illusions of the early postwar period when we believed that the world, so sorely tried by its great ordeal, would find peace and understanding as the reward of victory. They were years, too, when we grew in wisdom and in experience as we struggled to adapt our thoughts and our ways to the new role of world leadership into which we had been so suddenly placed.

These speeches are the record of the man who led his people—and much of the world—during this fateful decade. Though they were given to many diverse groups, they deal with variations on a single theme: Peace. With a devotion to peace, born out of long experience with war and a passionate conviction of the need for its abandonment, the President sought again and again to point out the requisites for peace and the means by which they could be achieved. The aggregate impact of these addresses is impressive particularly because the President endeavored constantly to detach essential principles and problems from the context of special circumstance and to subject them to thoughtful analysis.

Much stress is laid upon the fundamental need for responsible citizenship and a strong sense of civic obligation on the part of all our people. "Whatever America hopes to bring to pass in the world must first come to pass in the heart of America." This sentence from the First Inaugural, repeated in later addresses, clearly states one of the President's strong convictions. Coupled with it is a profound belief in the importance of Faith, a Faith arising from the Christian ethic, a Faith in the dignity of Man, and a Faith —expressed through patriotism—in the tenets of a democratic and free society.

But the President is a practical man, and he knows that Faith and Moral Principle are not enough to assure peace. In this collection of speeches, he states repeatedly his beliefs about the proper principles of foreign policy and the means by which they must be implemented if America is to be secure in an uncertain world. Here is a clear voice of judgment based on long experience.

Two of these addresses will be singled out for particular notice by the discerning reader. The first is the Gabriel Silver Lecture delivered at Columbia in March, 1950. Less well known than his subsequent speeches as President of the United States, this address foreshadows with clarity and detail the thoughts and views of the man who was destined so soon thereafter to give up his academic post for wider responsibilities. In the light of later developments, his comments on the dangers and inadequacies of "summit" Conferences are particularly striking.

The second is the draft text of the address which he had

planned to give at Leningrad on the occasion of his visit to the Soviet Union. Firm in tone, patient in its emphasis upon the peace-loving attitudes of our people, and constructive in its approach, it is a remarkable document, and one can only regret that it could not have been allowed to reach the eyes and ears of the Soviet people. The contrast with the bellicose fulminations of Chairman Khrushchev in America is striking.

It is a privilege for the Columbia University Press to publish these thirty addresses. They deserve—and will have—a wide and thoughtful reading public. They are a record of the beliefs and hopes of a man who deserves much from the people he has served so well.

GRAYSON KIRK

Columbia University
in the City of New York
December, 1960

CONTENTS

PEACE WITH JUSTICE

WORLD PEACE—A BALANCE SHEET

ADDRESS AT COLUMBIA UNIVERSITY

NEW YORK, MARCH 23, 1950

On behalf of Columbia University, I thank Mr. Leo Silver for the generous gift that will make the Gabriel Silver Lecture on Peace a recurring feature of the University calendar. His endowment will permit us at regular intervals to call on selected individuals for reports on peace. Perhaps there will be added new strength to the philosophical and social foundations of peace, and a stronger light thrown on the hazards within the international economy that endanger its permanence. Possibly there will be launched new attacks on inequities and injustices in which lurk some of the causes of war.

Mr. Silver has established a worthy memorial to his father and we are grateful that he has chosen Columbia University as its home. On my own behalf, I want to thank him for the honor paid me in his request that I deliver this inaugural of the series. Without his intervention, I should not be so presumptuous as to appear in this role before a distinguished gathering of Columbia faculty and graduate students because you are, in our country, part of the great body especially qualified to be the architects of world peace.

To you that classification may seem exaggeration beyond any warrant of fact. Quite the contrary. Any man who underestimates the importance of the American teacher in world affairs is misleading himself. Under our system, high governmental policy expresses the considered will of the people, and the will of the people, in the last analysis, is compounded out of the convictions, the idealisms, the purposes fostered in the classrooms of the nation's schools. What you teach is what the country does.

I come before you solely as a witness of things that have happened and of the impressions those have made upon me.

For some years, I was in the thick of war and reconstruction after war. A war that—despite all its terrors, its destruction, its cost—was for the Allied Nations, a crusade in the best sense of an often misused word, a reconstruction after war that, despite its bickerings, its suppression of freedom in many places and its disheartening cynicism, has established in the political sphere at least temporary— even if teetering—balance. These years and these experiences have served to ripen and enlarge my devotion to peace. I trust that they have also served to sharpen my powers of perception and judgment of the factors which seem always to balk man's efforts to close forever the doors of the Temple of Janus.

In discussing war and peace, we incline to paint one all black and the other all white. We like to repeat "There never was a good war, or a bad peace." But war often has provided the setting for comradeship and understanding and greatness of spirit—among nations, as well as men— beyond anything in quiet days; while peace may be marked by, or may even be the product of, chicanery, treachery, and the temporary triumph of expediency over all spiritual values.

The pact of Munich was a greater blow to humanity than

the atomic bomb at Hiroshima. Suffocation of human freedom among a once free people, however quietly and peacefully accomplished, is more far-reaching in its implications and its effects on their future than the destruction of their homes, industrial centers, and transportation facilities. Out of rubble heaps, willing hands can rebuild a better city; but out of freedom lost can stem only generations of hate and bitter struggle and brutal oppression.

Nor can we forget that, as Professor Lyman Bryson of Teachers College recently said: "There are even greater things in the world than peace." By greater things, he meant the ideals, the hopes and aspirations of humanity; those things of the soul and spirit which great men of history have valued far above peace and material wealth and even life itself.

Without these values, peace is an inhuman existence. Far better risk a war of possible annihilation than grasp a peace which would be the certain extinction of free man's ideas and ideals.

Clearly it was a choice between these two extremes that the British people were forced to make back in the dark summer of 1940. Whatever may be history's final judgment on the total war record of that nation, her people in that dire season of fear and foreboding proved themselves heroic and mighty in their spiritual greatness.

Twenty miles beyond their South coast, thinly manned by men—and women—armed with little more than their own courage, there was arrayed an invasion force of stupendous military might, hardened and flushed by sweeps from the Vistula to the Atlantic, from the Arctic to the

Alps. Other members of the British Commonwealth of nations, though loyal, could do little to relieve the frightening crisis that suddenly faced the Mother Country.

In all Europe and Asia, from the Bay of Biscay far into the Pacific, men awaited the blow that would destroy the British. The multitude of millions that dwelled in those two continents—even those who lately were allies—had been corrupted into a conviction that material force was unfailingly greater than the spirit of free men.

Throughout most of the rest of the world, there seemed to be an appalling ignorance that the defeat of Britain would mean the eventual extinction of the freedom for ideas and ideals that her people had done so much to win and support for all mankind. So, in her hour of gravest trial she stood largely alone, another David to champion a righteous but apparently hopeless cause.

But the British spurned all offers of peace and their great leader asked for battle—on their beaches, in their towns, along the lanes of England. His faith was rewarded in the final and complete Allied victory of 1945.

Millions of Americans, who saw what the British endured: broken towns, years of austerity, staggering debts and near-destitution, must be witnesses all our lives to the greatness of spirit in that people. *Their decision* to fight on gave freedom a new lease on life and gave all free peoples more space in time to destroy a vicious dictator and regain an opportunity to work out an enduring peace.

Our memories are short indeed, or we have failed to read the lesson of that experience, if we in 1950 are fearful of the future and allow despair to paralyze our efforts to build a lasting peace.

By this allusion to the British record, I do not in any way belittle the wartime contributions of the allies, including Russia; nor dull one whit the sharp fact that victory over the enemy could *not* have been accomplished without the giant strength of a united America. I dwell on the British role in 1940 and thereafter for two reasons. First, there is a tendency among us today to write off our friends in the Western nations because they are weak in numbers and weapons. Second, there is a parallel tendency to measure a possible enemy solely by the area he rules and the manpower he controls.

Many of us, even among professional soldiers, too easily accept as unfailingly true Napoleon's cynical statement: "God is on the side of the heaviest battalions." Napoleon himself lived and ruled and fought by that dictum, but his reign from coronation to final exile was shorter by months than even Hitler's, his fellow believer in the dominance of force.

Because there is one towering force in the world that often seems bent upon engulfing as much territory and as many people as it can, a great many surrender their hopes for peace as curtly as they write off our friends in Western Europe. Such pessimism invites disaster. Such an attitude, if it were founded on reason, would mean that the handful of men who dictate the policy of the Soviet system also dictate the fate of this globe. To any one ready to study the history of yesterday and the facts of today, that is a repugnant absurdity.

Granted, at any moment some one powerful nation could choose to follow a policy of world conquest by war. Nevertheless, the world has seen so many examples of this that, today, such a war would imply either an incredible stupidity, weakness, disunity, and unreadiness on one side or a miscalculation equal to the insanity and moral guilt on the side of the predatory nation. Until war is eliminated from international relations, unpreparedness for it is well nigh as criminal as war itself.

What then is the nature of the peace that we seek? What are the characteristics that distinguish it? These questions must be answered, if we are to know our objective, calculate our distance from it, decide on the measures necessary to its attainment.

Almost certainly, most men would agree that peace, to merit the name, should possess a reasonable assurance of permanence, should be the product of co-operation between all major nations, and should be secure against arbitrary violation by any power or group of powers. It is apparent, however, that we constantly use the word *"peace"* in two senses which differ sharply. One is the peace of our dreams—a peace founded in noble impulses, universally shared. It is always the ideal, the pole star that guides us on the proper path. The other peace is *something* of an armed truce; but today a half-loaf is better than none. By the improvisations, expediencies, and agreements under which we strive to maintain a peace based as much upon force and power as upon concepts of justice and fair play, we hope to reach the point where this peace becomes the starting point of the *real* peace we seek.

But permanence, universality, and security cannot be achieved merely by covenant or agreement. Treaties are too often scraps of paper; in our age the signal for two World Wars was the callous repudiation of pacts and pledged word. There must be a universal urge of decency.

This fact compels the observation that they are thinking wishfully who pin their hopes of peace upon a single "high level" conference and a resulting paper that would bear the promise of governmental heads to observe all the rights of others. An agreement, though it should bear the seal and ribbon of every chancellery in the world, is worth no more than the confidence placed by each signer in the good faith and integrity of every other. We must sadly acknowledge that today such world-wide confidence does not exist.

By all means let us continue to confer, especially with the view and purpose of reaching the required level of mutual faith and confidence, or as a substitute, of developing practical and mutually enforceable measures and reciprocal arrangements calculated to lessen the danger of war. But, equally, let us not delude ourselves that establishment of real peace is merely a matter of Very Important Personages signing papers or "talking tough" in Paris, Geneva, Washington, and Tahiti.

It is obvious that an enduring world-wide and secure peace must be founded on justice, opportunity, and freedom for all men of good will; be maintained in a climate of international understanding and co-operation; to free from militaristic menace; and be supported by an accepted and respected police power representing all nations. Critical factors in the problem of building such a peace are the needs of a human society comprised of individuals; and, further, the needs of a human society that is divided into independent nations, each sovereign within its own borders and competing with all others to promote the interests of its own citizens, often at the expense of others. There are two sides to the coin of peace, the individual and the national; if one is defective the coin is spurious.

On the side of the individual, peace requires an international society that is free from vicious provocations to strife among men. These are rooted in inequities so glaring that, to those who suffer them, they seem to make attractive any alternative. The gamble of war lures the desperate, for even overwhelming defeat can hardly worsen their state; while victory, if it gives the survivors any improvement, will be worth its cost in blood. It is possible, even probable, that hopelessness among a people can be a far more potent cause of war than greed. War in such case is a symptom, not a disease.

On the collective side of the coin, peace requires an international society liberated from the threat of aggression by neighbor on neighbor, a threat forever present when one or more nations are committed to the building or maintenance of gigantic military machines. No sane man will challenge, under present circumstances, the need for defensive strength designed to secure against internal or external attack the independence and sovereignty of a free state. But the continued existence of even one purely offensive force—a force for which there is no apparent need based in the logic of self-defense—denies enduring peace to the world. Those who have spawned such a force must either eventually destroy it by demobilization and justification for the heavy cost already laid on their people; or use it, tacitly or actively, as a threat or as a weapon. There is no middle course.

Always it has been difficult to distinguish between offensive and defensive armaments. Advancing science has obliterated whatever qualitative differences that once existed; today even the atom bomb is included in defensive arsenals. But differences do exist—vital differences. They are found, partially, in the quantitative factor.

The world forms its own sound opinion of a nation's martial purposes, primarily by the size and combinations of armaments supported, and by their geographical disposition and estimated state of readiness. To be considered also is the record of the particular nation, the extent to which it observes the ordinary rules of decency, courtesy, fairness, and frankness in dealing with others.

It is by such combinations of standards that we must today classify the world's armaments. For America, with whose professional security forces I have been intimately associated for almost forty years, I bear witness to peaceful intent. In all those years, I have never heard an officer of the Army, the Navy or the Air Force, or any responsible official of government, advocate, urge, discuss or even hint at the use of force by this country in the settlement of any actual or potential international problem.

And here it seems appropriate, in view of my insistent belief that the world must finally disarm or suffer catastrophic consequences, to assert my conviction that America has already disarmed to the extent—in some directions even beyond the extent—that I, with deep concern for her *present* safety, could possibly advise, until we have certain knowledge that all nations, in concerted action, are doing likewise.

I might state here also that the Baruch plan for the control of the atomic bomb was not only evidence of our peaceful intent, but was the most generous action ever made by any nation, equivalent in its field to the Marshall Plan.

Moreover, without American leadership in the search, the pursuit of a just and enduring peace is hopeless. Nowhere in the world, outside this land, is there the richness of resources, stamina and will needed to lead what at times may be a costly and exhausting effort. But leadership cannot be exercised by the weak. It demands strength, the strength of this great nation when its people are united in purpose, united in a common fundamental faith, united in their readiness to work for human freedom and peace; this spiritual and economic strength, in turn, must be reinforced in a still armed world by the physical strength necessary for the defense of ourselves and our friends.

Only by deliberate lies can the propagandist, foreign or domestic, stretch our arms program into more than the reasonable posture for defense that General Washington urged on his countrymen. And the heads of state everywhere, even the most suspicious and fearful, know that it is below even that level. Our processes are open to the inspection of all; we spend hardly a dollar or add a platoon to the military establishment without long and public debate.

Our 20th century international record, the statistics of our military forces, and the open procedures of our political system, all provide proof of our peaceful purposes; they prove also that our support of programs, in which universal peace will be secure, is as honest as it is sturdy.

The two requisites to an enduring peace—the elimination of deep-seated incitements to strife and hopelessness, and the elimination of armament for aggression—are, or should be, within the realm of feasible attainment. But man can remake the face of his physical environment and can harness all the powers of the universe more easily, it seems, than he can learn control of his temper as a member of the international community. Nevertheless, those who term these twin requisites utopian and visionary are cut from the same bolt of cloth as those of an earlier day who claimed that epidemics were an inescapable companion to human existence and denounced the preachers of sanitation as balkers of God's will.

To prevent the crime of war, all nations and all ideologies can unite without sacrifice of principle. But lest self-interest in minor matters breed a carelessness toward the gravity of this problem, there is required unity of understanding concerning the facts of modern war. After the world-wide devastation that grows daily more possible, none may be able to distinguish between the victor and the vanquished of a future conflict. Confronted by that outcome to another World War, all of us, East and West, are in the same boat. The boat can be swamped in a series of atomic blasts; but, sustained by understanding of a common peril, it can also carry us through to final peace. Thus, the possibility of total destruction, terrible though it is, could be a blessing as all nations, great and small, for the first time in human history, are confronted by an inescapable physical proof of their common lot. Franklin's "If we don't hang together, we shall each hang separately," has its international application today. There is no prod so effective as a common dread; there is no binder so unifying.

And we know the formula of success: First, justice,

freedom, and opportunity for all men; Second, international understanding; Third, disarmament; Fourth, a respected United Nations.

First of all, justice among men can be attained only by
the universal and equitable satisfaction of human hungers
that are threefold in their nature because man is at once a
physical creature who must be clothed and fed and shel-
tered; a thinking being who is forever questioning and
must be answered or given the opportunity to find the
answers; a spiritual being within whom burn longings and
aspirations that cannot be quenched by all the goods of
this world. Starvation and hardship, ignorance and its evils,
oppression and discrimination are the fuel of war—the
raw materials of strife.

So far as the world's food is concerned, all peoples must
learn together to make proper use of the earth on which
we live. Hovering even now over our shoulders is a specter
as sinister as the atomic bomb because it could depopulate
the earth and destroy our cities. This creeping terror is
the wastage of the world's natural resources and, particularly, the criminal exploitation of the soil. What will it
profit us to achieve the H-bomb and survive that tragedy
or triumph, if the generations that succeed us must starve
in a world, because of our misuse, grown barren as the
mountains of the moon?

By every step that the nations take toward more productive and efficient use of land, toward better production
and distribution of food, toward raising the living standards
of even the least of the world's tribes; by every school
house that is built where none was before; by every plague
spot that is cleansed and made healthful; by every increase

in the sum of universally shared knowledge and the consequent increase in each man's mastery of his environment; by every measure that enlarges men's opportunity to develop all their talents and capacities—by that much we reduce the stockpile of grievance, injustice, and discontent on which war feeds.

You say in objection: "Those are fine words, but all history proves that as man has advanced in material and intellectual strength, wars have not lessened in frequency but have grown in the tragedy and terror of their impact."

To that objection I report: The unrest that has gripped the world is at least partially due to the failure of the more fortunate to realize that their own self-interest requires them to teach others the techniques of raising human standards of existence. Thus, ostentatious wealth in fortunate areas has occasioned bitterness and envy in other localities where these could have been eliminated at no greater cost than that involved in teaching man to make the best use of the material resources surrounding him.

By no means do I believe that the wealthy of this world can solve this great problem of disparity merely by sharing what they now possess with the less fortunate. What is needed is the knowledge and understanding, the technical progress, that will allow all men to make the best use of nature's bounty. Progress in this direction is already an announced American purpose. Past failures to do more in this line have provided the demagogues and the propagandists of history with much of the ammunition they have used; and the war maker is first of all a propagandist.

The nations now have the technical knowledge and skill to end some flagrant disparities. The same measures

that banished the scourge of cholera or of typhus or malaria
from the American city can largely banish all pestilence
from all the continents of the earth. The machines that
have released the peoples of the West from the age-old
drudgeries of a hand-to-mouth existence can liberate the
peoples of all lands whose bitter bread is earned in exhausted bodies and shortened lives. And, certainly, there
is no need for starvation at any spot in a world that is
glutted in so many places with crops, great beyond domestic needs, that must rot or be destroyed.

Here again we must not be discouraged by the inescapable slowness of world progress. However disappointing
may be the lack of speed, every new evidence of advance
brings immediate hope of a brighter tomorrow to millions;
and peoples hopeful of their domestic future do not use
war as a solution to their problems. Hope spurs humans
everywhere to work harder, to endure more now that
the future may be better; but despair is the climate of war
and death. Even America, without American optimism,
can accomplish nothing beyond the needs of each day.

Now, while we attack the physical evils, we must battle
the ignorance which permits them. And I mean not only
ignorance in the individual human being, but those attitudes, policies, and prejudices which balk the free exchange
between the nations of information and knowledge that
will make human living a more full expression of man's
dignity. No scrap of knowledge, whose only effect is to
make life better, should be denied any nation by any other
nation. Even the Soviets, living behind a curtain woven from
fear, could afford to work with the rest of us, *now*, for this

decent and human objective. Though we may be generous, we can still expect rebuffs and gibes. But there is always the chance and the hope that hostile governments will understand, over the years, the honesty of our motives and join with us in their realization. If or when they do, we will all profit and we, both West and East, will sleep easier of nights.

Another thing, the stresses and strains of fear are intensified in our day because everywhere the superstitions of materialism are increasing their holds on the minds of men. Hundreds of millions live within the Communist orbit where the official doctrine makes mankind the helpless pawn of economic forces.

But man's spiritual side is still the dominant one. No human, whatever his position in the social hierarchy or his job in the working economy, merits more respect than any other animal of the woods or fields unless we accept without reservation the brotherhood of man under the Fatherhood of God. If men are not creatures of soul, as well as of body, they are not better than the field mule, harnessed to the plough, whipped and goaded to work, cared for in the measure of his cost and value. But too often, today, we incline to describe the ultimate in human welfare as a mule's sort of heaven—a tight roof overhead, plenty of food, a minimum of work and no worries or responsibilities. So far have we strayed in our sense of values. Unless we rekindle our own understanding, can we hope to make Marxist devotees see that things of the spirit— justice, freedom, equality—are the elements that make important the satisfaction of man's creative needs? If I doubted that man is something more than mere educated animal I should personally be little concerned in the question of war or peace.

Even under the most propitious of circumstances, the obstacles to growth of understanding are legion in number and staggering in their mass. Hundreds of millions behind the Iron Curtain are daily drilled in the slogan: "there is no God, and religion is an opiate." But not all the people within the Soviet accept this fallacy; and some day they will educate their rulers, or change them. True enough, too, there are many places where men of one color seem bent on degrading men of another color, shearing them of their dignity and standing as fellow beings. But the human conscience comes gradually to recognize this injustice and men of good purpose will grasp at any reasonable solution to eliminate it.

We cannot, of course, attain perfection in human relations even within the smallest community, no matter how many laws we pass or policemen we hire. The rogue and the villain skulk on dark corners. But as we put street lamps on these corners so that decent folk may walk abroad after dark, so we can relight the lamps of brotherhood where they have been extinguished among men. Again we see that the fortunate will serve their own best interests by eliminating injustice and its consequent urge toward strife.

While we strive in this effort, which is primarily concerned with the living standards of individual human beings, we can break down at the same time many of the barriers of misunderstanding that exist among the nations. Misunderstanding among neighbors is perilous in the atomic age. Unreadiness by free nations for joint defensive action against an aggressor is only one of the evils that stem from it. Through these same misunderstandings there is certain to be suffered economic loss and therefore ineffectiveness in the satisfaction of human hungers. Worst of all, even the slightest misunderstanding among the nations not committed to communism is another chink in the defenses against an aggressive ideology which overlooks no opportunity to subvert and destroy. In the situation of 1950 it is crystal clear that self-interest and the common interests of free nations go hand in hand.

There is no need to remake the world, outside the Soviet system, in the likeness of the United States or any other country. What I do suggest is that we recognize that every culture developed in the world has been worked out by its possessors to meet the circumstances of their own environment. Each race and each nation can learn from every other. There is none so close to self-sufficiency that it can do without the help and co-operation of others; none so primitive that it has not amassed a wisdom that can possibly enlighten even the most advanced.

The free world has already committed itself to attainment of our two basic conditions for permanent peace—the satisfaction of human hungers and a climate of international understanding and good will. Much has been done toward their achievement. The transformation of the world thus far accomplished is at least half a miracle. Moreover, the spokesmen of the Soviets declare that they are dedicated to the same purpose. Parenthetically, I might add, if *their* methods succeed, it would be, to us, a complete miracle.

Nevertheless, all governments pay an equal lip service to the common purpose of satisfying human hungers and promoting international understanding. Everyone of them, if challenged, can point to laws and policies that are noble beyond criticism. Why, then, is not world peace automatically ours?

Simply because the positive elements in the construction of peace can be nullified by any powerfully armed nation, whose motives are suspect, unless all are committed to disarmament and there is some means of enforcing peace among them. All the sanitary safeguards ever designed will not secure a community against disease if the residents of one block flaunt them; and the violators will not be persuaded to amend their ways until health officers, backed by the police and the laws, enforce the ordinances.

When even one major power, surreptitiously or flagrantly, builds and maintains a military machine beyond the recognized needs of reasonable security, a war of aggression is a constant threat to peaceful nations. At the very least, these armaments become the gangster's gun—a notice that might and might alone shall serve as judge and jury and sheriff in the settling of international dispute. That is the only realistic interpretation since no government otherwise would squander its revenue or exhaust its economy on so sterile an enterprise. It is clear that international disarmament is essential to a stable, enduring peace.

In a disarmed world, should it be attained, there must be an effective United Nations, with a police power universally recognized and strong enough to earn universal respect. In it the individual nations can pool the power for policing the continents and the seas against *international* lawlessness and those acts which involve two or more nations in their *external* relations.

I do not subscribe to any idea that a world police force

or a world organization should be permitted entrance to
any nation for the purpose of settling disputes among its
citizens, or for exercising any authority not specifically
and voluntarily accorded by the affected nation. At this
stage of civilization's progress any effort to push to this
extreme the purpose of international law enforcement will
defeat legitimate objectives. National sovereignty and independence have been won by most at too great a cost
to surrender to an external agency such powers. But by
the establishment of a United Nations police of properly
defined and restricted but effective powers, no nation
would surrender one iota of its current national functions
or authority, for none, by itself, now possesses a shred of
responsibility to police the world. To an international
peace organization, a nation would give up nothing beyond
its equitable share in men and money. How this organization
is to be constituted or how it is to be controlled, has yet
to be worked out, but with the principles honestly accepted, the procedural problems would be easy of solution.

I have spoken thus briefly of these two elements in
world peace—disarmament and United Nations authority
—because they are in a manner corollaries or sequels to
the other two—justice, freedom, opportunity for all men
of good will; and a climate of mutual understanding and
co-operation among the nations. Progress is bound to come
from slow, evolutionary processes rather than from violent
revolution in national and individual thinking.

But it is especially important that we do not fall prey
to pessimism and defeatism. To describe the attitudes of
many of us toward the current international scene, I give
you the following quotation:

"It is a gloomy moment in history. Not for many years,

not in the lifetime of most men who read this paper has there been so much grave and deep apprehension: never has the future seemed so incalculable as at this time.

"In France the political cauldron seethes and bubbles with uncertainty; Russia hangs as usual a cloud, dark and silent upon the horizon of Europe; while all the energies, resources and influences of the British Empire are sorely tried and are yet to be tried more sorely.

"It is a solemn moment and no man can feel indifference —which happily no man pretends to feel—in the issue of events.

"Of our own troubles no man can see the end."

That, ladies and gentlemen, though so vividly descriptive of today, appeared in Harpers Weekly, Saturday, October 10, 1857. Possibly we are wrong when we fearfully conclude that for the first time in history the governments regard each other with fear and suspicion.

What, actually, is the outlook today? In my opinion, far better than most of us normally judge; the world of 1950 is a far brighter and better place than the world of 1850. Starvation is no longer endemic among many millions on every continent—China is the one tragic exception. Illiteracy has vastly diminished in the masses of almost every nation. In the West at least, there is a new and increased appreciation of spiritual values. Even Russia, despite its all-powerful police and purges, is for the average Russian a vast improvement compared to the Russia of 1850.

As to those countries outside the Curtain, I doubt that we can point to any era or any decade when there was as much intelligent comprehension of each other's purposes as now characterizes their relationships. And in the broader scope, the United Nations, however halting its progress may be, however much its sessions are torn by the jeers and vetoes from one sector, is a visible and working entity, substantial evidence of developing hopes and purposes, an earnest of better things to come.

All of us have come a long way in the past century; none of us should despair when we think of what our situation was, and our prospects, as recently as the summer of 1940. What then can be done now, by this University, by the United States, by the free peoples to further the cause of peace?

The University, since its removal to Morningside Heights, has become an international center whose graduates can be found on every continent and whose influence has been a leaven for physical progress, intellectual fellowship, and spiritual growth among all peoples. The purpose of this University, without oversimplification, can be epitomized in one phrase—the good of humanity.

We hope to build here on the campus a Nutrition Center in which the world's scientists will find concentrated all the knowledge, the tools, the facilities that will enable them to devise better, more productive and more effective techniques for the use of physical resources and the satisfaction of man's physical needs. We already have, and in every recent term we have further amplified, an Institute of International Affairs where we hope the political and social leaders of the world will find concentrated the materials, the information, the masses of data that will enable them to adjust the stresses and needs of one area to the strains and surpluses of another.

We hope to establish here a Chair for Peace, possibly an Institute. The purpose will be to study war as a tragic social phenomenon: its origins, its conduct, its impact, and particularly its disastrous consequences upon man's spiritual, intellectual and material progress. All this we should study in a scholarly atmosphere, free from emotional bias and the daily crises of public life. No American university, I am told, has ever undertaken this comprehensive task. For me, there is something almost shocking in the realization that, though many millions have been voluntarily donated for research in cancer of the individual body, nothing similar has been done with respect to the most malignant cancer of the world body—war.

We are presently engaged in a study of the Conservation of Human Resources—restricted, as of now, to the United States—but which will be of immeasurable benefit to all the world in furthering the dignity of man as a human being. Another hope is to conduct an exhaustive study into the ways and means of applying to every man's good, in today's intricate economy, *all* the resources of America, in such way as to maintain and enlarge every freedom that the individual has enjoyed under our system. There are other projects, under way or under discussion, that will take their places beside or even in front of these. Each of them will help Columbia University a little better to fulfill its purpose—the peace, freedom, and good of America, and, therefore, of humanity.

As citizens of the United States, you and I, and all Americans in every corner of our land, must be forever mindful that the heritage of America and the strength of America are expressed in three fundamental principles:

First, that individual freedom is our most precious possession; Second, that all our freedoms are a single bundle, all must be secure if any is to be preserved; Third, that freedom to compete and readiness to co-operate make our system the most productive on earth. Only within the framework of these principles can we hope to continue the growth that has marked our history. Only thus can our millions reach the fullness of intellectual, moral, and physical welfare that is justly ours, and avoid any risk of submission to the all-powerful state. Moreover, only thus can the world have any hope of reaching the millennium of world peace. For without the example of strength, prosperity, and progress in a free America, there is nothing to inspire men to victory in today's struggle between freedom and totalitarianism.

As friends of free people everywhere in the world, we can by our own example—our conduct in every crisis, real or counterfeit; our resistance to propaganda and passion; our readiness to seek adjustments and compromise of difference—we can by our own example ceaselessly expand understanding among the nations. We must never forget that international friendship is achieved through rumors ignored, propaganda challenged and exposed; through patient loyalty to those who have proved themselves worthy of it; through help freely given, where help is needed and merited. In this sense there is no great, no humble among us. In rights and in opportunity, in loyalty and in responsibility to ideals, we are and must remain equal. Peace is more the product of our day-to-day living than of a spectacular program, intermittently executed.

The best foreign policy is to live our daily lives in honesty, decency, and integrity; at home, making our own land a more fitting habitation for free men; and, abroad, joining with those of like mind and heart, to make of the world a place where all men can dwell in peace. Neither palsied by fear nor duped by dreams but strong in the rightness of our purpose, we can then place our case and cause before the bar of world opinion—history's final arbiter between nations.

INAUGURAL ADDRESS 1953

DELIVERED AT THE CAPITOL

WASHINGTON, D.C., JANUARY 20, 1953

My friends, before I begin the expression of those thoughts that I deem appropriate to this moment, would you permit me the privilege of uttering a little private prayer of my own. And I ask that you bow your heads.

Almighty God, as we stand here at this moment my future associates in the executive branch of government join me in beseeching that Thou will make full and complete our dedication to the service of the people in this throng, and their fellow citizens everywhere.

Give us, we pray, the power to discern clearly right from wrong, and allow all our words and actions to be governed thereby, and by the laws of this land. Especially we pray that our concern shall be for all the people regardless of station, race, or calling.

May co-operation be permitted and be the mutual aim of those who, under the concepts of our Constitution, hold to differing political faiths; so that all may work for the good of our beloved country and Thy glory. Amen.

My fellow citizens:

The world and we have passed the midway point of a century of continuing challenge. We sense with all our faculties that forces of good and evil are massed and armed and opposed as rarely before in history.

This fact defines the meaning of this day. We are summoned by this honored and historic ceremony to witness more than the act of one citizen swearing his oath of service, in the presence of God. We are called as a people to give testimony in the sight of the world to our faith that the future shall belong to the free.

Since this century's beginning, a time of tempest has seemed to come upon the continents of the earth. Masses of Asia have awakened to strike off shackles of the past. Great nations of Europe have fought their bloodiest wars. Thrones have toppled and their vast empires have disappeared. New nations have been born.

For our own country, it has been a time of recurring trial. We have grown in power and in responsibility. We have passed through the anxieties of depression and of war to a summit unmatched in man's history. Seeking to secure peace in the world, we have had to fight through the forests of the Argonne, to the shores of Iwo Jima, and to the cold mountains of Korea.

In the swift rush of great events, we find ourselves groping to know the full sense and meaning of these times in which we live. In our quest of understanding, we beseech God's guidance. We summon all our knowledge of the past and we scan all signs of the future. We bring all our wit and all our will to meet the question: How far have we come in man's long pilgrimage from darkness toward light? Are we nearing the light, a day of freedom and of peace for all mankind? Or are the shadows of another night closing in upon us?

Great as are the preoccupations absorbing us at home, concerned as we are with matters that deeply affect our livelihood today and our vision of the future, each of these domestic problems is dwarfed by, and often even created by, this question that involves all human kind.

This trial comes at a moment when man's power to achieve good or to inflict evil surpasses the brightest hopes and the sharpest fears of all ages. We can turn rivers in their courses, level mountains to the plains. Oceans and land and sky are avenues for our colossal commerce. Disease diminishes and life lengthens.

Yet the promise of this life is imperiled by the very genius that has made it possible. Nations amass wealth. Labor sweats to create, and turns out devices to level not only mountains but also cities. Science seems ready to confer upon us, as its final gift, the power to erase human life from this planet.

At such a time in history, we who are free must proclaim anew our faith.

This faith is the abiding creed of our fathers. It is our faith in the deathless dignity of man, governed by eternal moral and natural laws.

This faith defines our full view of life. It establishes, beyond debate, those gifts of the Creator that are man's inalienable rights and that make all men equal in His sight.

In the light of this equality, we know that the virtues most cherished by free people—love of truth, pride of work, devotion to country—all are treasures equally precious in the lives of the most humble and of the most exalted. The men who mine coal and fire furnaces and balance ledgers and turn lathes and pick cotton and heal the sick and plant corn—all serve as proudly, and as profitably, for America as the statesmen who draft treaties and the legislators who enact laws.

This faith rules our whole way of life. It decrees that

we, the people, elect leaders not to rule but to serve. It asserts that we have the right to the choice of our own work and to the reward of our own toil. It inspires the initiative that makes our productivity the wonder of the world. And it warns that any man who seeks to deny equality among all his brothers betrays the spirit of the free and invites the mockery of the tyrant.

It is because we, all of us, hold to these principles that the political changes accomplished this day do not imply turbulence, upheaval, or disorder. Rather this change expresses a purpose of strengthening our dedication and devotion to the precepts of our founding documents, a conscious renewal of faith in our country and in the watchfulness of a Divine Providence.

The enemies of this faith know no god but force, no devotion but its use. They tutor men in treason. They feed upon the hunger of others. Whatever defies them, they torture, especially the truth.

Here, then, is joined no argument between slightly differing philosophies. This conflict strikes directly at the faith of our fathers and the lives of our sons. No principle or treasure that we hold, from the spiritual knowledge of our free schools and churches to the creative magic of free labor and capital, nothing lies safely beyond the reach of this struggle.

Freedom is pitted against slavery; lightness against the dark.

The faith we hold belongs not to us alone but to the free of all the world. This common bond binds the grower of rice in Burma and the planter of wheat in Iowa, the shepherd in southern Italy and the mountaineer in the

Andes. It confers a common dignity upon the French soldier who dies in Indochina, the British soldier killed in Malaya, the American life given in Korea.

We know, beyond this, that we are linked to all free peoples not merely by a noble idea but by a simple need. No free people can for long cling to any privilege or enjoy any safety in economic solitude. For all our own material might, even we need markets in the world for the surpluses of our farms and our factories. Equally, we need for these same farms and factories vital materials and products of distant lands. This basic law of interdependence, so manifest in the commerce of peace, applies with thousandfold intensity in the event of war.

So we are persuaded by necessity and by belief that the strength of all free peoples lies in unity; their danger, in discord.

To produce this unity, to meet the challenge of our time, destiny has laid upon our country the responsibility of the free world's leadership.

So it is proper that we assure our friends once again that, in the discharge of this responsibility, we Americans know that we observe the difference between world leadership and imperialism; between firmness and truculence; between a thoughtfully calculated goal and spasmodic reaction to the stimulus of emergencies.

We wish our friends the world over to know this above all: we face the threat, not with dread and confusion, but with confidence and conviction.

We feel this moral strength because we know that we are not helpless prisoners of history. We are free men. We shall remain free, never to be proven guilty of the one capital offense against freedom, a lack of staunch faith.

In pleading our just cause before the bar of history and in pressing our labor for world peace, we shall be guided by certain fixed principles.

These principles are:

(1) Abhorring war as a chosen way to balk the purposes of those who threaten us, we hold it to be the first task of statesmanship to develop the strength that will deter the forces of aggression and promote the conditions of peace. For, as it must be the supreme purpose of all free men, so it must be the dedication of their leaders, to save humanity from preying upon itself.

In the light of this principle, we stand ready to engage with any and all others in joint effort to remove the causes of mutual fear and distrust among nations, so as to make possible drastic reduction of armaments. The sole requisites for undertaking such effort are that, in their purpose, they be aimed logically and honestly toward secure peace for all; and that, in their result, they provide methods by which every participating nation will prove good faith in carrying out its pledge.

(2) Realizing that common sense and common decency alike dictate the futility of appeasement, we shall never try to placate an aggressor by the false and wicked bargain of trading honor for security. Americans, indeed all free men, remember that in the final choice a soldier's pack is not so heavy a burden as a prisoner's chains.

(3) Knowing that only a United States that is strong and immensely productive can help defend freedom in our world, we view our Nation's strength and security as a trust upon which rests the hope of free men everywhere. It is

the firm duty of each of our free citizens and of every free citizen everywhere to place the cause of his country before the comfort, the convenience of himself.

(4) Honoring the identity and the special heritage of each nation in the world, we shall never use our strength to try to impress upon another people our own cherished political and economic institutions.

(5) Assessing realistically the needs and capacities of proven friends of freedom, we shall strive to help them to achieve their own security and well-being. Likewise, we shall count upon them to assume within the limits of their resources their full and just burdens in the common defense of freedom.

(6) Recognizing economic health as an indispensable basis of military strength and the free world's peace, we shall strive to foster everywhere, and to practice ourselves, policies that encourage productivity and profitable trade. For the impoverishment of any single people in the world means danger to the well-being of all other peoples.

(7) Appreciating that economic need, military security, and political wisdom combine to suggest regional groupings of free peoples, we hope, within the framework of the United Nations, to help strengthen such special bonds the world over. The nature of these ties must vary with the different problems of different areas.

In the Western Hemisphere, we enthusiastically join with all our neighbors in the work of perfecting a community of fraternal trust and common purpose.

In Europe, we ask that enlightened and inspired leaders of the Western nations strive with renewed vigor to make the unity of their peoples a reality. Only as free Europe unitedly marshals its strength can it effectively safeguard, even with our help, its spiritual and cultural heritage.

(8) Conceiving the defense of freedom, like freedom itself, to be one and indivisible, we hold all continents and peoples in equal regard and honor. We reject any insinuation that one race or another, one people or another, is in any sense inferior or expendable.

(9) Respecting the United Nations as the living sign of all people's hope for peace, we shall strive to make it not merely an eloquent symbol but an effective force. And in our quest for an honorable peace, we shall neither compromise, nor tire, nor ever cease.

By these rules of conduct, we hope to be known to all peoples.

By their observance, an earth of peace may become not a vision but a fact.

This hope—this supreme aspiration—must rule the way we live.

We must be ready to dare all for our country. For history does not long entrust the care of freedom to the weak or the timid. We must acquire proficiency in defense and display stamina in purpose.

We must be willing, individually and as a nation, to accept whatever sacrifices may be required of us. A people that values its privileges above its principles soon loses both.

These basic precepts are not lofty abstractions, far removed from matters of daily living. They are laws of spiritual strength that generate and define our material strength. Patriotism means equipped forces and a prepared citizenry. Moral stamina means more energy and more productivity, on the farm and in the factory. Love of liberty means the

guarding of every resource that makes freedom possible—
from the sanctity of our families and the wealth of our soil
to the genius of our scientists.

And so each citizen plays an indispensable role. The
productivity of our heads, our hands, and our hearts is the
source of all the strength we can command, for both the
enrichment of our lives and the winning of the peace.

No person, no home, no community can be beyond the
reach of this call. We are summoned to act in wisdom and
in conscience, to work with industry, to teach with persuasion, to preach with conviction, to weigh our every deed
with care and with compassion. For this truth must be clear
before us: whatever America hopes to bring to pass in the
world must first come to pass in the heart of America.

The peace we seek, then, is nothing less than the practice
and fulfillment of our whole faith among ourselves and in
our dealings with others. This signifies more than the stilling of guns, it is easing the sorrow of war. More than escape
from death, it is a way of life. More than a haven for the
weary, it is a hope for the brave.

This is the hope that beckons us onward in this century
of trial. This is the work that awaits us all, to be done with
bravery, with charity, and with prayer to Almighty God.

TOWARD A GOLDEN AGE
OF PEACE

ADDRESS BEFORE THE AMERICAN SOCIETY OF NEWSPAPER EDITORS

APRIL 16, 1953

In this spring of 1953 the free world weighs one question above all others: the chance for a just peace for all peoples.

To weigh this chance is to summon instantly to mind another recent moment of great decision. It came with that yet more hopeful spring of 1945, bright with the promise of victory and of freedom. The hope of all just men that moment too was a just and lasting peace.

The eight years that have passed have seen that hope waver, grow dim, and almost die. And the shadow of fear again has darkly lengthened across the world.

Today the hope of free men remains stubborn and brave, but it is sternly disciplined by experience. It shuns not only all crude counsel of despair but also the self-deceit of easy illusion. It weighs the chance for peace with sure, clear knowledge of what happened to the vain hope of 1945.

In that spring of victory the soldiers of the Western Allies met the soldiers of Russia in the center of Europe. They were triumphant comrades in arms. Their peoples shared the joyous prospect of building, in honor of their dead, the only fitting monument—an age of just peace. All these war weary peoples shared too this concrete, decent purpose: to guard vigilantly against the domination ever again of any part of the world by a single, unbridled aggressive power.

This common purpose lasted an instant and perished. The nations of the world divided to follow two distinct roads.

The United States and our valued friends, the other free nations, chose one road.

The leaders of the Soviet Union chose another.

The way chosen by the United States was plainly marked by a few clear precepts, which govern its conduct in world affairs.

First: No people on earth can be held, as a people, to be an enemy, for all humanity shares the common hunger for peace and fellowship and justice.

Second: No nation's security and well-being can be lastingly achieved in isolation but only in effective co-operation with fellow-nations.

Third: Any nation's right to a form of government and an economic system of its own choosing is *inalienable*.

Fourth: Any nation's attempt to dictate to other nations their form of government, is *indefensible*.

And fifth: A nation's hope of lasting peace cannot be firmly based upon any race in armaments but rather upon just relations and honest understanding with all other nations.

In the light of these principles the citizens of the United States defined the way they proposed to follow, through the aftermath of war, toward true peace.

This way was faithful to the spirit that inspired the United Nations: to prohibit strife, to relieve tensions, to banish fears. This way was to control and to reduce armaments. This way was to allow all nations to devote their energies and resources to the great and good tasks of healing the war's wounds, of clothing and feeding and housing the needy, of perfecting a just political life, of enjoying the fruits of their own free toil.

The Soviet government held a vastly different vision of the future.

In the world of its design, security was to be found, not in mutual trust and mutual aid but in *force:* huge armies, subversion, rule of neighbor nations. The goal was power superiority at all costs. Security was to be sought by denying it to all others.

The result has been tragic for the world and, for the Soviet Union, it has also been ironic.

The amassing of Soviet power alerted free nations to a new danger of aggression. It compelled them in self-defense to spend unprecedented money and energy for armaments. It forced them to develop weapons of war now capable of inflicting instant and terrible punishment upon any aggressor.

It instilled in the free nations—and let none doubt this— the unshakable conviction that, as long as there persists a threat to freedom, they must, at any cost, remain armed, strong, and ready for the risk of war.

It inspired them—and let none doubt this—to attain a unity of purpose and will beyond the power of propaganda or pressure to break, now or ever.

There remained, however, one thing essentially unchanged and unaffected by Soviet conduct: the readiness of the free nations to welcome sincerely any genuine evidence of peaceful purpose enabling all peoples again to resume their common quest of just peace.

The free nations, most solemnly and repeatedly, have assured the Soviet Union that their firm association has never had any aggressive purpose whatsoever. Soviet leaders, however, have seemed to persuade themselves, or tried to persuade their people, otherwise.

And so it has come to pass that the Soviet Union itself has shared and suffered the very fears it has fostered in the rest of the world.

This has been the way of life forged by eight years of fear and force.

What can the world, or any nation in it, hope for if no turning is found on this dread road?

The worst to be feared and the best to be expected can be simply stated.

The *worst* is atomic war.

The *best* would be this: a life of perpetual fear and tension; a burden of arms draining the wealth and the labor of all peoples; a wasting of strength that defies the American system or the Soviet system or any system to achieve true abundance and happiness for the peoples of this earth.

Every gun made, every warship launched, every rocket fired signifies, in the final sense, a theft from those who hunger and are not fed, those who are cold and are not clothed.

This world in arms is not spending money alone.

It is spending the sweat of its laborers, the genius of its scientists, the hopes of its children.

The cost of one modern heavy bomber is this: a modern brick school in more than thirty cities.

It is two electric power plants, each serving a town of 60,000 population.

It is two fine, fully equipped hospitals.

It is some fifty miles of concrete highway.

We pay for a single fighter plane with a half million bushels of wheat.

We pay for a single destroyer with new homes that could have housed more than 8,000 people.

This, I repeat, is the best way of life to be found on the road the world has been taking.

This is not a way of life at all, in any true sense. Under the cloud of threatening war, it is humanity hanging from a cross of iron.

These plain and cruel truths define the peril, and point the hopes that come with this spring of 1953.

This is one of those times in the affairs of nations when the gravest choices must be made, if there is to be a turning toward a just and lasting peace.

It is a moment that calls upon the governments of the world to speak their intentions with simplicity and with honesty.

It calls upon them to answer the question that stirs the hearts of all sane men: *is there no other way the world may live?*

The world knows that an era ended with the death of Joseph Stalin. The extraordinary thirty-year span of his rule saw the Soviet Empire expand to reach from the Baltic Sea to the Sea of Japan, finally to dominate 800 million souls.

The Soviet system shaped by Stalin and his predecessors was born of one World War. It survived with stubborn and often amazing courage a second World War. It has lived to threaten a third.

Now a new leadership has assumed power in the Soviet Union. Its links to the past, however strong, cannot bind it completely. Its future is, in great part, its own to make.

This new leadership confronts a free world aroused, as rarely in its history, by the will to stay free.

This free world knows, out of the bitter wisdom of experience, that vigilance and sacrifice are the price of liberty.

It knows that the defense of Western Europe imperatively demands the unity of purpose and action made possible by the North Atlantic Treaty Organization, embracing a European Defense Community.

It knows that Western Germany deserves to be a free and equal partner in this community and that this, for Germany, is the only safe way to full, final unity.

This is the kind of free world which the new Soviet leadership confronts. It is a world that demands and expects the fullest respect of its rights and interests. It is a world that will always accord the same respect to all others.

So the new Soviet leadership now has a precious opportunity to awaken, with the rest of the world, to the point of peril reached and to help turn the tide of history.

Will it do this?

We do not yet know. Recent statements and gestures of Soviet leaders give some evidence that they may recognize this critical moment.

We welcome every honest act of peace.

We care nothing for mere rhetoric.

We are only for sincerity of peaceful purpose attested by deeds. The opportunities for such deeds are many. The performance of a great number of them waits upon no complex protocol but upon the simple will to do them. Even a few such clear and specific acts, such as the Soviet Union's signature upon an Austrian treaty or its release of thousands of prisoners still held from World War II, would be impressive signs of sincere intent. They would carry a power of persuasion not to be matched by any amount of oratory.

This we do know: a world that begins to witness the rebirth of trust among nations *can* find its way to a peace that is neither partial nor punitive.

With all who will work in good faith toward such a peace, we are ready, with renewed resolve, to strive to redeem the near-lost hopes of our day.

The first great step along this way must be the conclusion of an honorable armistice in Korea.

This means the immediate cessation of hostilities and the prompt initiation of political discussions leading to the holding of free elections in a united Korea.

It should mean, no less importantly, an end to the direct and indirect attacks upon the security of Indochina and Malaya. For any armistice in Korea that merely released aggressive armies to attack elsewhere would be a fraud.

We seek, throughout Asia as throughout the world, a peace that is true and total.

Out of this can grow a still wider task—the achieving of just political settlements for the other serious and specific issues between the free world and the Soviet Union.

None of these issues, great or small, is insoluble—given only the will to respect the rights of all nations.

Again we say: the United States is ready to assume its just part.

We have already done all within our power to speed conclusion of a treaty with Austria, which will free that country from economic exploitation and from occupation by foreign troops.

We are ready not only to press forward with the present plans for closer unity of nations of Western Europe but also, upon that foundation, to strive to foster a broader European community, conducive to the free movement of persons, of trade, and of ideas.

This community would include a free and united Germany, with a government based upon free and secret elections.

This free community and the full independence of the East European nations could mean the end of the present unnatural division of Europe.

As progress in all these areas strengthens world trust, we could proceed concurrently with the next great work: the reduction of the burden of armaments now weighing upon the world. To this end we would welcome and enter into the most solemn agreements. These could properly include:

1. The limitation, by absolute numbers or by an agreed international ratio, of the sizes of the military and security forces of all nations.

2. A commitment by all nations to set an agreed limit upon that proportion of total production of certain strategic materials to be devoted to military purposes.

3. International control of atomic energy to promote its use for peaceful purposes only and to insure the prohibition of atomic weapons.

4. A limitation or prohibition of other categories of weapons of great destructiveness.

5. The enforcement of all these agreed limitations and prohibitions by adequate safeguards, including a practical system of inspection under the United Nations.

The details of such disarmament programs are manifestly critical and complex. Neither the United States nor any other nation can properly claim to possess a perfect, immutable formula. But the formula matters less than the faith, the good faith without which no formula can work justly and effectively.

The fruit of success in all these tasks would present the world with the greatest task and the greatest opportunity of all. It is this: the dedication of the energies, the resources, and the imaginations of all peaceful nations to a new kind of war. This would be a declared total war, not upon any human enemy but upon the brute forces of poverty and need.

The peace we seek, founded upon decent trust and cooperative effort among nations, can be fortified, not by weapons of war but by wheat and by cotton, by milk and by wool, by meat and by timber and by rice. These are words that translate into every language on earth. These are needs that challenge this world in arms.

This idea of a just and peaceful world is not new or strange to us. It inspired the people of the United States to initiate the European Recovery Program in 1947. That program was prepared to treat, with like and equal concern, the needs of Eastern and Western Europe.

We are prepared to reaffirm, with the most concrete evidence, our readiness to help build a world in which all peoples can be productive and prosperous.

This Government is ready to ask its people to join with all nations in devoting a substantial percentage of the savings achieved by disarmament to a fund for world aid and reconstruction. The purposes of this great work would be to help other peoples to develop the undeveloped areas of the world, to stimulate profitable and fair world trade, to assist all peoples to know the blessings of productive freedom.

The monuments to this new kind of war would be these: roads and schools, hospitals and homes, food and health.

We are ready, in short, to dedicate our strength to serving the *needs*, rather than the *fears*, of the world.

We are ready, by these and all such actions, to make of the United Nations an institution that can effectively guard the peace and security of all peoples.

I know of nothing I can add to make plainer the sincere purpose of the United States. I know of no course, other than that marked by these and similar actions, that can be called the highway of peace.

Again we say: the hunger for peace is too great, the hour in history too late, for any government to mock men's hopes with mere words and promises and gestures.

The test of truth is simple. There can be no persuasion but by deeds.

Is the new leadership of the Soviet Union prepared to use its decisive influence in the Communist world, including control of the flow of arms, to bring not merely an expedient truce in Korea but genuine peace in Asia?

Is it prepared to allow other nations, including those of Eastern Europe, the free choice of their own forms of government?

Is it prepared to act in concert with others upon serious disarmament proposals to be made firmly effective by stringent UN control and inspection?

If not, where then is the concrete evidence of the Soviet Union's concern for peace?

The test is clear.

There is, before all peoples, a precious chance to turn the black tide of events. If we failed to strive to seize this chance, the judgment of future ages would be harsh and just.

If we strive but fail and the world remains armed against itself, it at least need be divided no longer in its clear knowledge of who has condemned humankind to this fate.

The purpose of the United States, in stating these proposals, is simple and clear.

These proposals spring, without ulterior purpose or political passion, from our calm conviction that the hunger for peace is in the hearts of all peoples—those of Russia and of China no less than of our own country.

They conform to our firm faith that God created men to enjoy, not destroy, the fruits of the earth and of their own toil.

They aspire to this: the lifting, from the backs and from the hearts of men, of their burden of arms and of fears, so that they may find before them a golden age of freedom and of peace.

PEACE BEGINS WITH THE INDIVIDUAL

ADDRESS AT THE SIXTH NATIONAL ASSEMBLY

OF THE UNITED CHURCH WOMEN, NATIONAL COUNCIL

OF THE CHURCHES OF CHRIST

ATLANTIC CITY, OCTOBER 6, 1953

At the outset of my talk, I should like to express, first, my appreciation of the honor I feel in speaking before this assemblage. An invitation to occupy this platform would confer distinction upon any man—perhaps I should say any mere man; for you are gathered here in high purpose, inspired by an unshakeable faith in yourselves, in your country, and in your God.

I can hardly hope that my words can further your purpose or deepen your threefold faith.

That faith, immeasurable and imponderable, daily exemplified in millions of American families, is the prime strength of our great nation. It is the very basis of our society. And it is the most heartening support for those whose obligation is to represent you in the conduct of national affairs, and community affairs.

Though I cannot enhance the spiritual wealth that is yours, perhaps I can, by identifying some of the circumstances of today that emphasize the value of this faith, encourage you to spread its influence into every human activity in every community across our land.

Now, of course, the cynic—the Marxist, or the worshipper of machines and numbers—will scoff that faith is no armor against artillery, that the spirit weakens fast before the blast of the bomb. But your husbands and brothers and fathers can testify that in the terrifying nakedness of the battlefield, the faith and the spirit of men are the keys to survival and victory.

Faith is evidently too simple a thing for some to recognize its paramount worth. Yet the present and the future demand men and women who are firm in their faith in our country and unswerving in their service to her. This is true in every basic unit of our political and social life: in the family, the community, the State, and the Nation.

This audience peculiarly symbolizes the smallest and the most important of these units—the American family. We of America have always recognized that the soundness of our Nation depends primarily upon the quality of our home and family life.

While our homes have witnessed scarcely any of the horrors of the battlefield that are so familiar to citizens of Western Europe, we know that our former unique physical security has almost totally disappeared before the long-range bombers and the destructive power of a single bomb.

Today we are face to face with the most extraordinary physical development of all time—the application of nuclear fission and nuclear fusion to the world's armaments.

These discoveries in the field of science present in themselves no threat to man. Like other scientific developments, they are susceptible to good or evil use, depending upon the intent of the individual or group possessing them.

The mysteries of the atom are known to Russia. Russia's

hostility to free government, and to the religious faith on which free government is built, is too well known to require recital here. It is enough for us to know that even before Russia had this awesome knowledge, she by force gained domination over six hundred million peoples of the earth. She surrounded them with an Iron Curtain that is an effective obstacle to all intellectual, economic, and spiritual intercourse between the free world and the enslaved world. Now, of these two worlds, the one is compelled by its purpose of world domination, the other by its unbreakable will to preserve its freedom and security to devote these latest discoveries of science to increasing its stockpiles of destructive armaments.

Man's greatest scientific achievement, therefore, cannot yet be made exclusively to serve the advancement of man's welfare and happiness. Instead we are forced to concentrate on building such stores of armaments as can deter any attack against those who want to be free.

Men of faith everywhere must gain a broader understanding of these potentials, both destructive and constructive.

We must certainly make sure that all the world comprehends, in simplest terms, the paramount alternatives of our day. The first of these alternatives is a wasteful and devastating contest in the production of weapons of inconceivable power. The other alternative is a world ever advancing in peace and prosperity through the co-operative effort of its nations and peoples.

The choice that spells terror and death is symbolized by a mushroom cloud floating upward from the release of the mightiest natural power yet uncovered by those who search the physical universe. The energy that it typifies is, at this state of human knowledge, the unharnessed blast. In its wake we see only sudden and mass destruction, erasure of cities, the possible doom of every nation and society.

This horror must not be.

This titanic force must be reduced to the fruitful service of mankind.

This can come to pass only as one of the results of shaping a firm and just and durable peace.

Such a peace cannot be achieved suddenly by force, by edict, or by treaty. It can come only slowly and tortuously. It will not be won by dark threats or glittering slogans. It will be born only of courage, knowledge, patience, leadership.

To strive faithfully for this peace, even as our science constantly develops new methods of mass destruction, imposes upon us a host of intricate labors. We and our friends in the free world must build, maintain, and pay for a military might assuring us reasonable safety from attack. From this position of secure confidence, we must seek to know and respond to the legitimate aspirations and hopes of all peoples. We must arrange trade systems that will provide each with the necessaries of life and opportunity for self-advancement. We must seek to understand and resolve age-old prejudices, ambitions, and hatreds that still scar great parts of the whole world. And they must be removed, or at least ameliorated. We must provide machinery and techniques to encourage that peaceful communication and mutual confidence which alone can finally lift the burden of arms from the backs of men.

Now, these are some of the grand labors before us—the tasks and tests and problems that span the world.

For the spirit that will resolve them, however, we need not seek the source in distant places.

I deeply believe that one of the supreme hopes for the world's destiny lies in the American community: in its moral values, in its sense of order and decency, in its co-operative spirit.

We know—and all the world constantly reminds us— that the future well-being of humanity depends directly upon America's leadership.

I say emphatically that this leadership depends no less directly upon the faith, the courage, the love of freedom, and the capacity for sacrifice of every American citizen, every American home, every American community.

I wish there were words of mine that could bring this truth home more certainly to each of us. I do not mean merely or only that our government and our leadership is the product of the qualities of each of us multiplied by 160 million. I mean more, this: the example we give the world when we talk about noble virtues that are necessary if civilization is to attain that future for which it was designed, and for which obviously the Almighty intended.

We speak of sacrifice. If each of us would search our own memories; how often have we, as we urged economy upon government, local city and state, urged that something not be given to us? "Don't build us a new post office; we don't need it; ours is good enough. Build it for the other city. Don't give me free postage, make me pay for what it costs to carry the letter."

What I am trying to get at is that America's policies abroad, to have any force, must be the reflection of the attitudes and qualities displayed by our people. No individuals

—no group of individuals—however brilliant, however eloquent, can possibly do any effective work in leading the world toward peace unless back of them is the mightiest force yet developed on God's footstool, and that is the force of a united America; an America determined to do real and constructive work.

This means then, that there is a clear and compelling answer to the question in the hearts of all of us: How can we better fit ourselves to be worthy of freedom, to guard its virtues, to enjoy its bounty?

That answer is: by making each life, each home, each community more worthy of the trust it bears for all mankind.

This worthiness will come in the measure that we show ourselves truly convinced that the central facts of human life are human freedom, human rights, human obligations; all expressing that human dignity which is a reflection of man's divine origin and destiny.

Our purpose is to grow even beyond the golden dreams of our forebears in material wealth, in intellectual stature, in spiritual strength. But to do so, each citizen and every community must match the founders of this nation in fiery independence, confident optimism, sturdy self-reliance, and we must sustain that capacity for conquering difficulties that has always been a quality of America.

With this spirit, each of you—each of us—like, indeed, every American citizen can arouse your own community to renewed awareness of the promise of freedom.

With your neighbors, you can join in work that even as it remakes your own town or hamlet helps remake the world.

For it is within your power to reach for and to attain that

day when you and all your neighbors can proudly say:

"These things, here, in this community are faithful to freedom.

"Here in this town, our public schools are staffed and equipped to train our children splendidly, to be free and responsible citizens."

Not so long ago, I met with a small group of people, and their purpose was to complain to me about certain things in our public school system. They directed some criticism at school teachers, and what these teachers thought—their policies, the philosophy they were teaching.

I asked this group one question only. "You recognize a teacher's great opportunity for influencing your children's future, for the planting of good thoughts or bad thoughts, for the teaching of a sound philosophy, or one that is based on falsity. Have you had that teacher in your home? Have you had her, or him, to dinner? Have you taken the trouble to find out for yourself what is the philosophy of these people to whom you are entrusting the most priceless possession you have, your children?"

"Now," I said, "many people have not been hesitant to join the ranks of the critics and say these teachers are not doing a good job. Then why haven't you done your part of the job: brought them in, talked to them, to see whether you could straighten them out, or get ones of which you approved?"

What I am trying to bring home is that as we see difficulties and defects in the body politic, in the social order, we must never attempt before our own consciences to dodge our own responsibilities.

And so we can say that, "Our teachers, loyal citizens to

their free country, enjoy true freedom of thought, untrammeled by political fashion or expediency."

And we should go on and be able to say, "Here in this city our libraries contain everything that can add to man's enlightenment and understanding—respecting common decency but disdaining any other censorship.

"Here our ministers and Sunday school teachers command the respect that they so justly earn in teaching our sons and our daughters the love of the Almighty.

"Here our hospitals and our clinics give faithful care to all who are sick and cannot help themselves.

"Here in this community, our people, all our people, have the chance to enjoy the arts, to learn, to become intimate friends with the heritage of freedom.

"Here we rely, not primarily upon government grant or political panacea, but upon our own wisdom and industry to bring us the good and comforting things of life.

"Here we know not the sight or smell of slums that choke the spirit of men.

"Here all of us work to make our processes of government the best, the most honest and the most just, known to any man.

"Here we have welcomed with our hearts new citizens from distant lands, and here we thank them for the strength they have added to our own.

"Here there is true equality of opportunity for work, for education, for enjoyment of all freedom's blessings. For we know that whatever we have and hold is the work and the treasure of men of all races and color and creeds.

"Here, in this community, in short, any free man can be proud to live."

All that I have tried to express to you rests upon one truth in which I firmly believe. I tried to speak it on the day last January when I took the oath of office as President of the United States. That truth is:

"Whatever America hopes to bring to pass in the world, must first come to pass in the heart of America."

I know of no more plain or pure ideal to which we can pledge our lives.

I know of no other way we can prove worthy of freedom.

ART OF PEACE

ADDRESS BEFORE THE GENERAL ASSEMBLY OF THE
UNITED NATIONS, DECEMBER 8, 1953

When Secretary General Hammarskjold's invitation to address this General Assembly reached me in Bermuda, I was just beginning a series of conferences with the Prime Ministers and Foreign Ministers of Great Britain and of France. Our subject was some of the problems that beset our world.

During the remainder of the Bermuda Conference, I had constantly in mind that ahead of me lay a great honor. That honor is mine today as I stand here, privileged to address the General Assembly of the United Nations.

At the same time that I appreciate the distinction of addressing you, I have a sense of exhilaration as I look upon this Assembly.

Never before in history has so much hope for so many people been gathered together in a single organization. Your deliberations and decisions during these somber years have already realized part of those hopes.

But the great tests and the great accomplishments still lie ahead. And in the confident expectation of those accomplishments, I would use the office which, for the time being, I hold, to assure you that the Government of the United States will remain steadfast in its support of this body. This we shall do in the conviction that you will provide a great share of the wisdom, the courage, and the faith which can bring to this world lasting peace for all nations, and happiness and well being for all men.

Clearly, it would not be fitting for me to take this occasion to present to you a unilateral American report on Bermuda. Nevertheless, I assure you that in our deliberations on that lovely island we sought to invoke those same great concepts of universal peace and human dignity which are so cleanly etched in your Charter.

Neither would it be a measure of this great opportunity merely to recite, however hopefully, pious platitudes.

I therefore decided that this occasion warranted my saying to you some of the things that have been on the minds and in the hearts of my legislative and executive associates for a great many months, thoughts I had originally planned to say primarily to the American people.

I know that the American people share my deep belief that if a danger exists in the world, it is a danger shared by all, and equally, that if hope exists in the mind of one nation, that hope should be shared by all.

Finally, if there is to be advanced any proposal designed to ease even by the smallest measure the tensions of today's world, what more appropriate audience could there be than the members of the General Assembly of the United Nations?

I feel impelled to speak today in a language that in a sense is new. One which I, who have spent so much of my life in the military profession, would have preferred never to use.

That new language is the language of atomic warfare.

The atomic age has moved forward at such a pace that every citizen of the world should have some comprehension, at least in comparative terms, of the extent of this development, of the utmost significance to every one of us. Clearly, if the peoples of the world are to conduct an intelligent search for peace, they must be armed with the significant facts of today's existence.

My recital of atomic danger and power is necessarily stated in United States terms, for these are the only incontrovertible facts that I know. I need hardly point out to this Assembly, however, that this subject is global, not merely national in character.

On July 16, 1945, the United States set off the world's first atomic explosion.

Since that date in 1945, the United States of America has conducted forty-two test explosions.

Atomic bombs today are more than twenty-five times as powerful as the weapons with which the atomic age dawned, while hydrogen weapons are in the ranges of millions of tons of TNT equivalent.

Today, the United States' stockpile of atomic weapons, which, of course, increases daily, exceeds by many times the explosive equivalent of the total of all bombs and all shells that came from every plane and every gun in every theatre of war in all of the years of World War II.

A single air group, whether afloat or land-based, can now deliver to any reachable target a destructive cargo exceeding in power all the bombs that fell on Britain in all of World War II.

In size and variety, the development of atomic weapons has been no less remarkable. The development has been such that atomic weapons have virtually achieved conventional status within our armed services. In the United States, the Army, the Navy, the Air Force, and the Marine Corps are all capable of putting this weapon to military use.

But the dread secret, and the fearful engines of atomic might, are not ours alone.

In the first place, the secret is possessed by our friends and allies, Great Britain and Canada, whose scientific genius made a tremendous contribution to our original discoveries and designs of atomic bombs.

The secret is also known by the Soviet Union.

The Soviet Union has informed us that, over recent years, it has devoted extensive resources to atomic weapons. During this period, the Soviet Union has exploded a series of atomic devices, including at least one involving thermonuclear reactions.

If at one time the United States possessed what might have been called a monopoly of atomic power, that monopoly ceased to exist several years ago. Therefore, although our earlier start has permitted us to accumulate what is today a great quantitative advantage, the atomic realities of today comprehend two facts of even greater significance.

First, the knowledge now possessed by several nations will eventually be shared by others, possibly all others.

Second, even a vast superiority in numbers of weapons, and a consequent capability of devastating retaliation, is no preventive, of itself, against the fearful material damage and toll of human lives that would be inflicted by surprise aggression.

The free world, at least dimly aware of these facts, has naturally embarked on a large program of warning and defense systems. That program will be accelerated and expanded.

But let no one think that the expenditure of vast sums for weapons and systems of defense can guarantee absolute safety for the cities and citizens of any nation. The awful arithmetic of the atomic bomb does not permit of any such easy solution. Even against the most powerful defense, an aggressor in possession of the effective minimum number of atomic bombs for a surprise attack could probably place a sufficient number of his bombs on the chosen targets to cause hideous damage.

Should such an atomic attack be launched against the United States, our reactions would be swift and resolute. But for me to say that the defense capabilities of the United States are such that they could inflict terrible losses upon an aggressor; for me to say that the retaliation capabilities of the United States are so great that such an aggressor's land would be laid waste—all this, while fact, is not the true expression of the purpose and the hope of the United States.

To pause there would be to confirm the hopeless finality of a belief that two atomic colossi are doomed to malevolently eye each other indefinitely across a trembling world. To stop there would be to accept helplessly the probability of civilization destroyed—the annihilation of the irreplaceable heritage of mankind handed down to us generation from generation—and the condemnation of mankind to begin all over again the age-old struggle upward from savagery toward decency, and right, and justice.

Surely no sane member of the human race could discover victory in such desolation. Could anyone wish his name to be coupled by history with such human degradation and destruction.

Occasional pages of history do record the faces of the "Great Destroyers" but the whole book of history reveals mankind's never-ending quest for peace, and mankind's God-given capacity to build.

It is with the book of history, and not with isolated pages, that the United States will ever wish to be identified. My country wants to be constructive, not destructive. It wants agreements, not wars, among nations. It wants itself to live in freedom, and in the confidence that the people of every other nation enjoy equally the right of choosing their own way of life.

So my country's purpose is to help us move out of the dark chamber of horrors into the light, to find a way by which the minds of men, the hopes of men, the souls of men everywhere, can move forward toward peace and happiness and well being.

In this quest, I know that we must not lack patience.

I know that in a world divided, such as ours today, salvation cannot be attained by one dramatic act.

I know that many steps will have to be taken over many months before the world can look at itself one day and truly realize that a new climate of mutually peaceful confidence is abroad in the world.

But I know, above all else, that we must start to take these steps—NOW.

The United States and its allies, Great Britain and France, have over the past months tried to take some of these steps. Let no one say that we shun the conference table.

On the record has long stood the request of the United States, Great Britain, and France to negotiate with the Soviet Union the problems of a divided Germany.

On the record has long stood the request of the same three nations to negotiate an Austrian State Treaty.

On the same record still stands the request of the United Nations to negotiate the problems of Korea.

Most recently, we have received from the Soviet Union what is in effect an expression of willingness to hold a Four Power Meeting. Along with our allies, Great Britain and France, we were pleased to see that this note did not contain the unacceptable preconditions previously put forward.

As you already know from our joint Bermuda communique, the United States, Great Britain, and France have promptly agreed to meet with the Soviet Union.

The Government of the United States approaches this conference with hopeful sincerity. We will bend every effort of our minds to the single purpose of emerging from that conference with tangible results toward peace—the only true way of lessening international tension.

We never have, we never will, propose or suggest that the Soviet Union surrender what is rightfully theirs.

We will never say that the peoples of Russia are an enemy with whom we have no desire ever to deal or mingle in friendly and fruitful relationship.

On the contrary, we hope that this Conference may initiate a relationship with the Soviet Union which will eventually bring about a free intermingling of the peoples of the East and of the West—the one sure, human way of developing an understanding required for confident and peaceful relations.

Instead of the discontent which is now settling upon Eastern Germany, occupied Austria, and the countries of Eastern Europe, we seek a harmonious family of free European nations, with none a threat to the other, and least of all a threat to the peoples of Russia.

Beyond the turmoil and strife and misery of Asia, we

seek peaceful opportunity for these peoples to develop their natural resources and to elevate their lives.

These are not idle words or shallow visions. Behind them lies a story of nations lately come to independence, not as a result of war, but through free grant or peaceful negotiation. There is a record, already written, of assistance gladly given by nations of the West to needy peoples, and to those suffering the temporary effects of famine, drought, and natural disaster.

These are deeds of peace. They speak more loudly than promises or protestations of peaceful intent.

But I do not wish to rest either upon the reiteration of past proposals or the restatement of past deeds. The gravity of the time is such that every new avenue of peace, no matter how dimly discernible, should be explored.

There is at least one new avenue of peace which has not yet been well explored: an avenue now laid out by the General Assembly of the United Nations.

In its resolution of November 18th, 1953, this General Assembly suggested: "that the Disarmament Commission study the desirability of establishing a sub-committee consisting of representatives of the Powers principally involved, which should seek in private an acceptable solution . . . and report on such a solution to the General Assembly and to the Security Council not later than 1 September 1954."

The United States, heeding the suggestion of the General Assembly of the United Nations, is instantly prepared to meet privately with such other countries as may be "principally involved," to seek "an acceptable solution" to the atomic armaments race which overshadows not only the peace, but the very life, of the world.

We shall carry into these private or diplomatic talks a new conception.

The United States would seek more than the mere reduction or elimination of atomic materials for military purposes.

It is not enough to take this weapon out of the hands of the soldiers. It must be put into the hands of those who will know how to strip its military casing and adapt it to the arts of peace.

The United States knows that if the fearful trend of atomic military buildup can be reversed, this greatest of destructive forces can be developed into a great boon, for the benefit of all mankind.

The United States knows that peaceful power from atomic energy is no dream of the future. That capability, already proved, is here—now—today. Who can doubt, if the entire body of the world's scientists and engineers had adequate amounts of fissionable material with which to test and develop their ideas, that this capability would rapidly be transformed into universal, efficient, and economic usage.

To hasten the day when fear of the atom will begin to disappear from the minds of people and the governments of the East and West, there are certain steps that can be taken.

I therefore make the following proposals:

The Governments principally involved, to the extent permitted by elementary prudence, to begin now and continue to make joint contributions from their stockpiles of normal uranium and fissionable materials to an International Atomic Energy Agency. We would expect that such an agency would be set up under the aegis of the United Nations. The ratios of contributions, the procedures and other details would properly be within the scope of the "private conversations" I have referred to earlier.

The United States is prepared to undertake these explorations in good faith. Any partner of the United States acting in the same good faith will find the United States a not unreasonable or ungenerous associate.

Undoubtedly initial and early contributions to this plan would be small in quantity. However, the proposal has the great virtue that it can be undertaken without the irritations and mutual suspicions incident to any attempt to set up a completely acceptable system of world-wide inspection and control.

The Atomic Energy Agency could be made responsible for the impounding, storage, and protection of the contributed fissionable and other materials. The ingenuity of our scientists will provide special safe conditions under which such a bank of fissionable material can be made essentially immune to surprise seizure.

The more important responsibility of this Atomic Energy Agency would be to devise methods whereby this fissionable material would be allocated to serve the peaceful pursuits of mankind. Experts would be mobilized to apply atomic energy to the needs of agriculture, medicine, and other peaceful activities. A special purpose would be to provide abundant electrical energy in the power-starved areas of the world. Thus the contributing powers would be dedicating some of their strength to serve the needs rather than the fears of mankind.

The United States would be more than willing; it would

be proud to take up with others "principally involved" the development of plans whereby such peaceful use of atomic energy would be expedited.

Of those "principally involved" the Soviet Union must, of course, be one.

I would be prepared to submit to the Congress of the United States, and with every expectation of approval, any such plan that would:

First, encourage world-wide investigation into the most effective peacetime uses of fissionable material, and with the certainty that they had all the material needed for the conduct of all experiments that were appropriate;

Second, begin to diminish the potential destructive power of the world's atomic stockpiles;

Third, allow all peoples of all nations to see that, in this enlightened age, the great powers of the earth, both of the East and of the West, are interested in human aspirations first, rather than in building up the armaments of war;

Fourth, open up a new channel for peaceful discussion, and initiate at least a new approach to the many difficult problems that must be solved in both private and public conversations, if the world is to shake off the inertia imposed by fear, and is to make positive progress toward peace.

Against the dark background of the atomic bomb, the United States does not wish merely to present strength, but also the desire and the hope for peace.

The coming months will be fraught with fateful decisions. In this Assembly; in the capitals and military headquarters of the world; in the hearts of men everywhere, be they governors or governed, may they be the decisions which will lead this world out of fear and into peace.

To the making of these fateful decisions, the United States pledges before you, and therefore before the world, its determination to help solve the fearful atomic dilemma; to devote its entire heart and mind to find the way by which the miraculous inventiveness of man shall not be dedicated to his death, but consecrated to his life.

PROPAGANDA AND TRUTH

ADDRESS AT THE AMERICAN NEWSPAPER

PUBLISHERS ASSOCIATION DINNER

NEW YORK, APRIL 22, 1954

The responsibilities and the constructive influence of the American press make this a significant occasion to me; one that I welcome. From personal experience, in war and in peace, I have come to recognize your dedication to truth and to the welfare of your country. You deserve the applause of free men, everywhere.

You are, of course, cosmopolitan in thought and in character, at least I am quite well aware, after sitting between the St. Louis Post-Dispatch and the Minneapolis Star and Tribune, that you are not members of a one-party press.

Eight years ago, almost to the day, I addressed the Bureau of Advertising. At that moment, the horror of war was a bitter memory of the recent past. A revulsion against war or any reminder of war possessed our people. The atmosphere was charged with emotionalism that could have destroyed our military strength. Fortunately, our newspapers did not then permit us, nor are they now permitting us, to forget the ever-present reality of aggressive threat.

Aggression is still a terrible reality, though on all the continents and the islands of the earth, mankind hungers for peace. This universal hunger must be satisfied.

Either the nations will build a co-operative peace or, one

by one, they will be forced to accept an imposed peace, now sought by the Communist powers, as it was by Hitler.

But free men still possess the greater portion of the globe's resources and of the potential power to be produced from those resources. They possess scientific skill, intellectual capacity, and sheer numbers in excess of those available to the Communist world. Consequently, free men can have a co-operative peace, if with hearts and minds cleansed of fear and doubt, together they dedicate themselves to it in unity and in understanding and in strength.

It is urgent that we try to clarify our thinking about the prospect. Let us start with our own present position. This nation is a marvel of production, rich in total wealth and individual earnings; powerful in a unique combination of scientific, military, economic, and moral strength. For generations our country has been free from the devastation of war in her homeland and is blessed with staunch and friendly neighbors. We covet no nation's possessions. We seek only the friendship of others. We are eager to repay this priceless gift in the same coin.

Surely, the United States, by all the standards of history, should possess a genuine peace and tranquility.

But our Nation today is not truly tranquil. We, her people, face a grave danger which, in essence at least, all of us understand. This danger, this peril calls for two far-reaching policies or purposes behind which all in our country should be solidly united. They are:

First, all our efforts must be bent to the strengthening of America in dedication to liberty; in knowledge and in comprehension; in a dependable prosperity widely shared; and in an adequate military posture.

Second, this strength—all of it—must be devoted to the building of a co-operative peace among men.

Those are the fixed purposes of the vast majority of our people. But in a world of ideological division, competitive rivalry, turbulent crisis in one place and political upheaval in another, their achievement demands far more than good intentions or glowing words.

If we are to build and maintain the strength required to cope with the problems of this age, we must co-operate one with the other, every section with all others, each group with its neighbors. This means domestic unity, about which I talk incessantly. Unity does not imply rigid conformity to every doctrine or position of a particular political figure. But it does require a common devotion to the cardinal principles of our free system; shared knowledge and understanding of our own capacities and opportunities; and a common determination to co-operate unreservedly in striving toward our truly important goals. This type of unity is the true source of our great energy—our spiritual, intellectual, material, and creative energy.

Futhermore, our people, strong and united, must co-operate with other nations in helping build a co-operative peace. Such co-operation requires the American people to increase their understanding of their fellowmen around the globe. Likewise, the nations beyond our shores must come to understand better the American people, particularly our hopes and our purposes. And, because of the relatively greater stake we have in world stability, because history has decreed that responsibility of leadership shall be placed upon this nation, we must take the initiative in the development of that genuine international understanding on which a co-operative peace must be built.

In these truths I find my justification for this appearance before you. The increase of understanding and knowledge is a task that cannot be accomplished solely by our schools or our churches or from political platforms. The malignant germs of misunderstanding and misinformation are at work in the minds of men twenty-four hours of every day. To combat them challenges the sturdy, and the effort of every individual who occupies any position of influence on public opinion.

Every newspaper, every magazine, every radio, and television station has the mission of bringing home to all our people and to as many other people of the world as we can reach, the facts of existence today. But this is not enough.

Every agency of human communication also must help people everywhere achieve perspective with respect to facts. Suppose the American press should faithfully report the details of every crime committed in our country, but should be invariably silent on the apprehension and punishment of criminals. Would there not soon be created a universal impression of national lawlessness, disorder, and anarchy? Facts must be related one to the other in truthful perspective. Only within such framework shall we reach clear decisions in the waging of the continuous struggle for a stronger America, and a peaceful world.

Domestic unity and strength as well as international understanding depend, therefore, in great part, on the free flow of information, and its balanced presentation.

I am not suggesting that the cause of domestic unity would

be served by any attempt of yours to slant the news, or to turn your news columns into editorials. The consequent loss of public respect and confidence would soon destroy the influence of the press. But I do believe most earnestly that the press should give emphasis to the things that unite the American people equal to that it gives to the things that divide them.

News of events which divided may be more spectacular than news of developments which unify. But a free press can discharge its responsibility to free people only by giving all the facts in balance. Facts in perspective are vital to valid citizen judgments. Sound judgment is crucial to the preservation of freedom. Hence a free press can sustain itself only by responsibly reporting all the facts and ideas: the spectacular and the unspectacular, the unifying facts and the divisive.

Could not reader-understanding be as powerful a criterion in newspaper offices as reader-interest?

Need these two qualities be incompatible? I think not. Certainly, the great journalists of our day, in critically examining and reporting on a legislative proposal must inevitably deal with such constructive questions as:

Does it or does it not tend to sustain our economy; to provide needed military strength; to increase our understanding of others or others' understanding of us? Does it give us a more secure position internationally? Does it promise to preserve and nurture love of liberty and self-dependence among our people? Does it improve our health and our living standards? Does it insure to our children the kind of nation and government we have known?

If proposed laws and policies are described as mere battle

grounds on which individuals or parties seeking political power suffer defeat or achieve victory, then indeed is the American system distorted for us and for the world. If the fortunes of the individual supporting or opposing a measure become, in our public accounts, as important as the principle or purpose of the project and its effect upon the nation, then indeed are we failing to develop the strength that understanding brings. If the day comes when personal conflicts are more significant than honest debate on great policy, then the flame of freedom will flicker low indeed.

I trust you do not view my remarks as an attempt to tell you how to run your own business. I am, however, willing to take the risk of your misinterpretation. James Madison once wrote: "A popular government without popular information or the means of acquiring it is but a prologue to a farce or a tragedy or perhaps both." So we are talking of a problem that the responsible governmental official cannot ignore, just as none of you can close your eyes to it.

We are not moving toward farce or tragedy. But knowledge of the facts and of their interrelationships is more than ever essential to the solution of human problems.

I know that to present the facts in perspective is a difficult task. The haste of living creates reader-impatience. It discourages complete explanation, and places a premium upon cliches and slogans. We incline to persuade with an attractive label; or to damn with a contemptuous tag.

But catchwords are not information. And, most certainly, sound popular judgment cannot be based upon them.

On the steady day-by-day dissemination of complete information depends our people's intelligent participation in their own government. For them that is no light thing.

The decisions they must make are crucial in character and world wide in scope. On them depend all the necessities and comforts of life, from the amount of money in their pocketbooks, the pavement on their highways, the housing in their towns, to the sort of country they will leave behind as a heritage to their children. They need full and accurate information. Newspapers can give it to them. On every question where they have it, their decisions will be sound.

If increased knowledge and understanding are necessary to promote the unity of our people, they are equally necessary to the development of international co-operation. At this juncture in world affairs, ignorance of each other's capacities, hopes, prejudices, beliefs, and intentions can destroy co-operation and breed war.

Nowhere on this planet today is there an impregnable fortress, a continent or island so distant that it can ignore all the outer world. If this is not to be the age of atomic hysteria and horror, we must make it the age of international understanding and co-operative peace. Even the most rabid Marxist, the most ruthless worshipper of force, will in moments of sanity admit that. International understanding, however, like domestic unity, depends in large part on the free full flow of information and its balanced presentation.

But recent reports state that seventy-five percent of all the people who inhabit the earth live under censorship. Illiteracy affects vast numbers in many areas of the globe. And, of course, there are language and cultural barriers. Understanding cannot, under these circumstances, be easily or quickly achieved. Into the vacuum caused by censorship and illiteracy, pours the positive and poisonous propaganda of the Soviets. For twenty-four hours each day, it pours in.

The Communist propaganda machine for instance, tirelessly tells all the world that our free enterprise system inevitably must collapse in mass unemployment, industrial strife, financial bankruptcy. Time and again, Communistic propaganda has shifted and reversed its tactics. But this one charge is firmly fixed in the party line from Marx to Malenkov.

Our United States Information Service, co-operating with similar efforts by friendly nations, seeks to combat propaganda with truth. Every dollar we put into it, when wisely used, will repay us dividends in the triumph of truth and the building of understanding. But our official Information Service is properly limited in purpose, as it is in size. The mass information, of us and to us, must flow through the established publicity media of the several nations. Of all these we think ours the best and the most efficient.

Yet, a study in which, I am told, many of you co-operated, shows that the average daily newspaper in the United States prints about four columns a day of news stories from abroad. I do not know whether that is too little, too much, or about right. But I do know that in this amount of daily space it is hard to inform the American people about relevant happenings in all other countries.

Two-thirds of this foreign news was found to be about important official ceremonies and events in other countries; about their internal political crises, their foreign relations involvements, their official statements and pronouncements. Very little of the news had to do with the man in the street, or with his social, educational, cultural, civic, and religious life and history. Yet an understanding of these is indispensable to an understanding of a nation.

The same specialists who studied this question also examined many European newspapers. There, too, news about the average American was scant. Those among you who have spent years abroad have undoubtedly been amazed by the frequency with which misleading or distorted opinions of our individual and national life are expressed by citizens of other countries.

It is always disconcerting to hear foreign friends speaking disparagingly of the American civilization as a collection of shiny gadgets. It is alarming to know that we are considered so immature in world politics as to be ready to provoke a war needlessly and recklessly. It is even worse to learn that we are often judged as power-hungry as the men in the Kremlin.

Because of a tragic failure to understand us and our purposes, the citizen of Western Europe frequently looks upon America and the U.S.S.R. as two great power complexes, each seeking only the most propitious moment in which to crush the other by force. He believes also that, in the meantime, each seeks alliances with nations throughout Europe with the sole purpose of using them as pawns when the moment of crisis arrives. We know that we seek only peace, by co-operation among equals. Success in the great purpose requires that others likewise know this, also.

As individuals we are frequently pictured abroad as rich, indifferent to all values other than money, careless of the rights of others and ignorant of the contributions others have made to the progress of Western civilization.

Undoubtedly these misconceptions are partially the result of Communist propaganda. But they flourish in the lack of comprehensive, truthful two-way information.

Here at home we need fuller and better information of others, if we are wisely to direct our policies toward real security. Many of us incorrectly assume that all other countries would like to live under a system identical or similar to ours. Some believe that all foreigners are lazy or decadent, that few pay taxes, that they hate us for the sole reason that we are prosperous. We hear often that the people of a particular nation are cowardly, or have no love of country, or pride in their citizenship. Too often we think of them as physically weak, intellectually shallow, and spiritually defeated.

Of course, there are individuals everywhere who fit these descriptions. But it is dangerous to us and to peace when we carelessly speak in generalities of this kind, characterizing an entire nation.

We live in a small world, and only by a co-operative effort of the free peoples occupying important areas can we build security and peace. It is not a question of turning the press, radio, television, and newsreels into media of sugar-coated propaganda, "selling" America to the Frenchman, France to the German, and Britain to the American.

It is quite different from that. I repeat: for understanding we need the facts and the perspective within which they fit. I am sure that the free press in all free countries has made real progress in this direction. But I think a lot more can, and by all means should, be done. The future of all of us depends upon it.

No group can be more effective in such accomplishment than you of the American Newspaper Publishers Association. Here, indeed, is an endeavor worthy of your talents and skills.

Within the framework of friendly alliances, we are joined with hundreds of millions among the free nations in working agreements, primarily concerned with military security, but inescapably dealing with every hope and every concern of daily life. Together we live in a mighty arena, bounded by the polar regions, practically encircling the globe, peopled by men and women of independent nations. These peoples, with scanty information and understanding of one another, are now allies of convenience under Communist threat; but tomorrow they could be full partners permanently joined in mutual understanding, impelled by common aspirations. Among the nations of that vast arena, at least, war can become unthinkable—quickly. A co-operative peace among them is no mirage of the dreamer.

Within the United Nations, we possess a global forum where we can plead the cause of peace so that even the men of the Kremlin must listen. Their ears may be stopped to the spirit of our words. Their minds, however, cannot forever be shut to the facts of the age within which we, and they, must live physically separated one from the other by a few hours of flight.

We cannot hope with a very few speeches, a few conferences, a few agreements to achieve the most difficult of all human goals—a co-operative peace for all mankind. Here may I say, my friends, that your representatives in the diplomatic world have no other thought or no other purpose than that which I have just stated: the achievement of a co-operative peace among the free nations and eventually to enlarge that by appealing to the common sense, representing the facts of the world as they are today to all others, so that even the iron wall must crumble and all men can join together.

To lead that kind of effort, we are blessed—and I say we are blessed, and I believe it from the bottom of my heart—with a man whose whole life has been devoted to this one purpose, who from babyhood has studied and thought and contemplated how to achieve this one great goal of human kind, well knowing that within his lifetime perfection cannot be attained, but to do his part in reaching it. I cannot tell you how sincerely I believe that every one of us, every one of 160 million people, owes a great debt of gratitude to Foster Dulles.

Free men do not lose their patience, their courage, their faith, because the obstacles are mountainous, the path uncharted. Given understanding, they invariably rise to the challenge.

Never, then, has there been a more compelling and rewarding time to work for international understanding, to labor for co-operative peace.

I most firmly believe that the American people's decision to strengthen our country in moral leadership, in intellectual stature, in military posture, in a dependable prosperity widely shared will be realized. Underlying that decision is a tremendous spiritual energy which I believe to be adequate to every test. I believe that it grows from day to day as our people become more and more aware of the deadly nature of the world's struggle.

I most firmly believe, too, that world leadership in the cause of co-operative peace lies within the capacity of America. This capacity will be realized when everyone uses his mind and his will and all his resources in union with others of like influence to bring about the understanding, the comprehension, the determination we need. Freedom of expression is not merely a right in the circumstances of today, its constructive use is a stern duty. Have we, have you as publishers, the courage to fully exercise the right and perform the duty?

Along with patriotism—understanding, comprehension, determination are the qualities we now need. Without them, we cannot win. With them, we cannot fail.

THE IDEAL OF PEACE

ADDRESS AT THE AMERICAN JEWISH TERCENTENARY

OCTOBER 20, 1954

We have come together in memory of an inspiring moment in history. That moment, three hundred years ago, when a small band of Jewish people arrived on the ship *Saint Charles* in what was then the Dutch colony or state of New Amsterdam. It was an event meaningful not only to the Jews of America, but to all Americans of all faiths, of all national origins.

On that day there came to these shores twenty-three people whose distant ancestors had, through the Old Testament, given new dimensions of meaning to the concepts of freedom and justice, of mercy and righteousness, kindness and understanding. Ideas and ideals which were to flower on this continent. They were of a people who had done much to give to Western civilization the principle of human dignity; they came to a land which would flourish beyond all seventeenth century dreams because it fostered that dignity among its citizens.

Of all religious concepts, this belief in the infinite worth of the individual is beyond doubt among the most important. On this faith our forefathers constructed the framework of our Republic.

In this faith in human dignity is the major difference between our own concept of life and that of enemies of freedom. The chief among these enemies a decade and more ago were Nazi and Fascist forces which destroyed so many of our fellow men. Today the Communist conspiracy is the principal influence that derides the truth of human worth and, with atheistic ruthlessness, seeks to destroy the free institutions established on the foundation of that truth.

Asher Levy and his party came to this land on that day long ago because even then they had to find a country where they could safely put into practice their belief in the dignity of man.

In this respect, as in so many others, they were no different from scores of other groups that landed on our shores. Only thirty-four years earlier, another party had landed at Plymouth Rock. That group, too, came here in the hope of escaping persecution, of gaining religious freedom, of settling quietly in the wilderness to build their homes and rear their families.

And there was another noble concept of our common Judeo-Christian civilization shared by these two groups: the ideal of peace.

I recall that wonderful prophecy of Isaiah: "And the work of righteousness shall be peace; and the effect of righteousness, quietness and assurance forever."

The pursuit of peace is at once our religious obligation and our national policy. Peace in freedom where all men dwell in security is the ideal toward which our foreign policy is directed.

My friends, I have been thrilled this evening by the historical accounts we have heard of the adventures of those twenty-three people. That was three hundred years ago. That is approximately ten generations. Now I want to look forward this evening, instead of back. And I want to give you some little conception of what I believe our responsibility to those of three hundred years hence is.

If you, each of you, would assume no inter-marriage whatsoever among your progenitors for those ten generations, do you realize that each of you was produced by 1,024 people of ten generations ago?

If you invert that pyramid and throw your mind forward ten centuries, you can see the enormous number of people that are going to be directly related to you, perhaps if you were so fortunate, and your responsibility to them, and to all their friends and neighbors.

So I think it is only fitting that while we have heard this saga of the adventures of these twenty-three people and their origins, that if you will allow me to talk a little bit about the hopes and aims of your government in beginning now the movement toward what we hope will be a far better world three hundred years from now, that would be the thing I would like to do this evening.

I know that I am speaking to people who deeply love peace. I know that with all other Americans you share a profound thanksgiving that for the first time in twenty years there has been for some months no active battlefield anywhere in the world.

Moreover, while fighting has been brought to a halt during the past twenty-one months, still other developments favorable to the maintenance of peace have been brought about. This has been done through understanding and through persistent and patient work in which your government has been a helpful participant. Some of these developments have commanded our headlines: Korea, Egypt, Trieste, Iran, Guatemala.

Our people and their government are dedicated to making this a just and a lasting peace.

In the years immediately ahead, the advancement of peace will demand much of us, our strength, our patience, our wisdom, our will. It will demand, above all, a realistic comprehension of the world and of its challenging problems. Some of the factors in these problems are new, and some old.

The principal and continuing factor is the persistently aggressive design of Moscow and Peiping, which shows no evidence of genuine change despite their professed desire to relax tensions and to preserve peace. Continuing, also, is the breadth and scope of the Communist attack; no weapon is absent from their arsenal, whether intended for destruction of cities and people or for the destruction of truth, of integrity, or loyalty.

The major new factor in the world today, beside the absence of fighting, is the rapid development in military weapons. Weapons that in total war would threaten catastrophe. These products of science alone should be sufficient to stimulate the genuine efforts of all, including the Kremlin, to give to the world a true and permanent peace.

For our part we shall explore every avenue toward that goal. With any and all who demonstrate honesty of purpose, we are happy to confer. But well we realize that in the circumstances of the moment America must remain strong, and the community of free nations must likewise remain strong to discourage the use of force in the world. In this effort, we must help to harmonize the divergent views of the many free, self-governing nations, and without encroaching upon rights which all people cherish. For in the diversities of freedom are a tremendous might, a might which the imposed system of Communism can never match.

Our nation, because of its productivity and power, both existing and potential, holds a prime responsibility for maintaining peace. How, then, shall we meet this responsibility? With what policies can we best pursue our goal of peace?

Certain fundamentals are clear. Our nation does not covet the territory of any people. We have no wish to dominate others. The peace we seek is a secure and a just peace, not bought at the expense of others, not bought at the expense of principle, and not bought by abject surrender of our vital interests. Peace so bought would at best be an illusion, and at worst a permanent loss of all that we hold most dear.

The following avenues must be trod as we make our way toward our peaceful goal.

First, we must tirelessly seek, through the United Nations, through every other available avenue open to us, every means to establish the conditions for an honorable peace.

Second, we must promote the unity and collective strength of other free peoples.

Third, we must maintain enough military strength to deter aggression and so promote peace.

Now, in these thoughts, we Americans overwhelmingly agree.

To examine briefly the first principal avenue, we stand ready to join all others in removing fear among nations. We shall resolutely adhere to the principles of the United Nations Charter. We shall constantly urge the Communist rulers to do the same. We shall keep open the existing channels of negotiations, and shall use them whenever there is any prospect of positive results.

At the Berlin and Geneva Conferences, our nation sought serious negotiation on German unity, on a treaty for Austria, and on a political settlement for Korea. Our efforts found no similar response from the Communist side. We will not be misled by proposals intended to divide the free nations and to delay their efforts to build their own defenses. Nevertheless, no matter how discouraging the prospect, no matter how intractable the Communist regimes, we shall press on our search for agreement.

We will welcome a workable system for limiting armaments and controlling atomic energy. Moreover, if the armaments burden can be lifted, this government stands ready to ask the Congress to redeem the pledge I made a year ago last April, to help support, from the funds thus saved, a world-wide development program.

Now, the second road leading toward our peaceful goal concerns our efforts to strengthen and unify other free peoples.

To meet the challenge destiny has laid upon our country, we must strive to help these free peoples achieve their own security and well-being; we must encourage regional groupings of these peoples; we must ourselves foster and practice policies that encourage profitable trade and productivity in the free world.

In these areas, there has been heartening progress. We have broadened our alliances. We have helped to remove sources of conflict. We have helped to build firmer foundations for social and economic progress in our quest for peace.

For some years free world nations have sought to associate the Federal Republic of Germany in the Atlantic Community. Rejection of the European Defense Treaty by the French Assembly seven weeks ago was a setback to that hope. Yet, no nation in Western Europe was willing to accept this setback as final. In the recent meetings at London, the free Western nations reasserted their basic unity and established a new pattern for achieving their common purposes. Then Secretary of State Dulles has just joined our European allies in Paris in further important negotiations to strengthen European co-operation.

In southeast Asia, we have sought united action to preserve for the free countries of that area the independence accorded them since the end of World War II. Unfortunately, in recent years no foundation had been laid for effective united action to prevent Communist gains. Because of their consequent isolation, the governments that bore the burden of the Indochina war understandably sought its conclusion in the face of the limitless manpower of China.

But recently at Manila we succeeded in negotiating a treaty with Asian and European countries. This pact symbolizes the desire of these nations to act together against aggression and to consult together on measures against subversion. The Manila pact, bringing together states of the East and the West, and the related Pacific Charter are a long step toward the peaceful progress to which all Asian peoples aspire, whether or not members of that Pact.

Perhaps you would allow me to pause here to say, I have traveled this world in peace and war, and there is one fact to which I can testify with the greatest confidence: all peoples want peace—all peoples. The misunderstandings that keep us apart seem to be of our own making, the making of government, and of selfishness in leaders. Basically, the heart of the people seems to have a similarity, wherever you find the people.

In this Hemisphere, we have strengthened our solid understandings with our American neighbors. At the Caracas Conference earlier this year, the American Republics agreed that if international communism were to gain control of the political institutions of any one American state, that this control would endanger them all, and therefore would demand collective action. Recently such a threat arose in Guatemala. The American states were preparing to act together to meet it when the Guatemalans themselves removed the danger. The Caracas agreement will stand as a bulwark of freedom in the Western Hemisphere.

In a number of areas throughout the free world, dangers to peace have been eliminated. The problem of Trieste, a threat to peace for a decade, has now been satisfactorily solved by Italy and Yugoslavia, with friendly assistance from the United States and Great Britain. Egypt and Britain have reached an amicable adjustment of questions centering on Suez. Iran has been helped in settling its difficult internal problems and is moving toward firm and friendly relations with the West.

In the Near East, we are all regretfully aware that the major differences between Israel and the Arab States remain unresolved. Our goal there, as elsewhere, is a just peace. By firm friendship toward Israel, and all other nations in that area, we shall continue to contribute to the peace of the world. But I assure you that, in helping to strengthen the security of the entire Near East, we shall make sure that any arms we provide are devoted to that purpose, not to creating local imbalances which could be used for intimidation of or aggression against any neighboring nation. In every arrangement—every arrangement—we make with any nation, there is ample assurance that this distortion of our purposes cannot occur.

The fact that so many stubborn problems have been re-solved through patience and forbearance surely justifies our hope that, by similar efforts, the nations of the free world will be able to eliminate other problems. Such efforts themselves tend to bring the free nations closer together. In speaking recently of the London Conference, Sir Winston Churchill said of his country and the United States, "True and friendly comprehension between our kindred nations has rarely reached a higher standard."

Since I personally have been in many conferences with my friend Sir Winston during the past twelve years on these subjects affecting the friendship between Britain and America, I can testify with him, and in spite of the differences that seem magnified at times in our public prints, that statement is true. Our relations with our British friends are solid and sound.

In addition, we must devise means by which more highly developed countries can assist peoples who face the difficulties of an earlier stage of economic development.

As we continue to assist in these efforts, we shall also contribute much to free world unity by the wise use of our great economic power. We have in the past provided indispensable assistance to our partners. We continue to stand ready to help; to repair the ravages of war; to ease economic difficulties caused by their efforts to build needed military strength for the good of all of us; to relieve disasters such as flood or famine.

Economic relations, however, are a two-way street. If the common goal is to be reached, free nations must subordinate the selfish to the general interest. All must bear their fair share of the common burden. All must do more to liberalize the exchange of goods among free peoples. Let us be mindful, of course, of our own responsibility in this field. Bold action could release powerful forces of economic enterprise from which the whole free world would benefit.

And if there were no other reason for national policy concerning itself every day and every minute with the nation's economy and full employment, it would be justified by the need for this kind of economic strength in meeting our world problems.

We must continue to explore ways in which nuclear discoveries can be turned to the service of man's peaceful needs. Since our nation's proposal for an international effort toward this end was laid before the United Nations last December, we have taken the initiative in this direction. We would welcome the participation of the Soviet Union. But this great effort for human welfare cannot wait upon their decision.

Our third major road leads us to maintain enough military strength to deter aggression and to help keep peace in the world.

This strength is a trust on which rests the current safety of free men.

Neither in size nor in character can our military establishment remain static. With constantly changing dangers, with rapidly changing developments in the science of warfare, our military forces, too, must change. From atomic submarine to atomic cannon, from new weapon systems to new military organizations, this giant complex structure must respond to the current needs of our time. Above all, its purpose is to prevent aggression and war. Our forces will never be used to initiate war against any nation; they will be used only for the defense of the free world.

Together with the armed strength of other free nations, our military power, the greatest in our peacetime history, is today a deterrent to war. This awesome power we must and shall maintain, for we are determined that at all times, in today's uncertain world, we shall be able to deal effectively and flexibly with whatever situations may arise.

In these many ways our nation will continue tirelessly in its quest for peace based on justice. In recent months, we have come far, and yet we know that the road ahead is long and difficult. But we shall continue to press on.

As we do so, we shall keep faith with those of earliest America who came to these shores three centuries and more ago. They launched a venture in freedom unparalleled in man's struggle over the ages. They sought peace and freedom and justice for themselves and for those who were to follow.

Yes, my friends, we know, with the prophet Isaiah, that the work of righteousness shall be peace.

Now let me remind you that when those people came, they didn't come for a negative purpose, just to be free of persecution. They sought the positive right to stand up as free men, as dignified humans; and the struggle that they carried forward to achieve those rights has been described to you eloquently and vividly this evening.

In the same way, in preserving peace in the world, international peace is not a static, is not a negative thing. It is a positive thing, of preparing the world, the conditions in the world, where people may live honorably and upright, and at peace.

And we know this: that as we labor for peace, we labor for all humanity, for all values, for all of enduring meaning to mankind. Never was there a nobler cause. Ringingly, insistently, it calls out to us, all of us, for ardent devotion and advocacy. To work with all our hearts for peace in the world is a task not alone for the soldier, the diplomat, the scholar, the statesman—peace is a job for every one of us, the concern of the working man, businessman, the clerk, the farmer, and doctor, and engineer, rabbi, clergyman, and priest, the teacher, the parent, and the child.

Let us then, each of us, resolve anew that we shall have peace. Let us then have faith that we shall succeed. Let us strive for peace with all our hearts and minds. From county seat to the conference table among nations; let us talk for peace from the classroom to the Congressional hall.

And my fellow citizens, let each of us pray for peace. Pray that He who rules over nation and man may guide every human being toward that wisdom and understanding that forever will bar from mankind the source of war.

THE DESIRE TO BE FREE

EXTRACT FROM AN ADDRESS TO THE

NATIONAL COUNCIL OF CATHOLIC WOMEN

BOSTON, NOVEMBER 8, 1954

Peace is the problem of the American people.

Of course, we would like, through some engagement—some conference—to accomplish all these things in a single day, or a single month. We have not eliminated tuberculosis and cancer, and other dread diseases of mankind in a month. We still labor. We don't give up.

I say with all the earnestness that I can command, that if American mothers will teach our children that there is no end to the fight for better relationships among the people of the world, we shall have peace. Because, as they do this, other mothers will do it; and gradually the age-old longing of humankind for peace will be reflected in better governmental structures, governmental structures that will be forced to comply with the demands of the great and enlightened citizenry throughout the world.

And so, far greater in importance to every American family than any of these activities I have been describing is the patient, tireless effort of our government to establish a just peace among nations.

Twelve years ago today, the first American troops landed in North Africa. I was in command of those troops in the European theatre, and on that day started the great ground conflict by American troops in Europe that did not end until Hitler was dead and Germany had surrendered. Now as we look back on that day, and on the most terrible war in human history, we again resolve that there must never be another war.

Today the fathers and mothers of our land rejoice that the possibility of permanent peace is more promising than at any time in recent years. They are grateful for the ending of bloodshed in Korea and Southeast Asia, the repulse of communism in Guatemala, the easing of tensions in Iran, Suez, and Trieste, and the promising agreement recently reached in Western Europe. They are heartened, too, by the building of strength where there was weakness throughout the Pacific. Despite such instances of provocation as that which occurred yesterday [On November 7, 1954 a United States Air Force RB-29 was shot down by Russian fighters.] off the coast of Japan, all of us are profoundly thankful that the terrible specter of war looms less threateningly over all mankind.

Now to convert this uneasy global armistice to a lasting peace, with justice for all people everywhere, is the longing of the parents of America's children. To attain this enduring peace, while living in freedom, must ever be the over-riding goal of our American foreign policy.

Without exciting fears or false hopes, without magnifying difficulties or dwelling upon mistakes, we must squarely face every obstacle to peace and attempt to overcome it. This means patience, courage, profound confidence in the common yearnings of the people of the world. This determination, this confidence, must become a spiritual and an

instinctive part of each American beginning at every
mother's knee.

Through the United Nations—through every possible
means—we must strive to build an honorable peace. I know
all Americans are hopeful that our proposal for an international pool of atomic energy will inaugurate a new phase in
negotiations between the United States and the Soviet
Union. I deeply believe that, regardless of the Soviet decision, the cause of peace will be furthered as we go ahead
with friendly nations to turn this new science to the arts of
peace.

At the same time, we must strive to maintain the collective,
united strength of free peoples. By broadening alliances, by
strengthening our cultural ties with peoples of other lands,
we build a firmer foundation for permanent peace throughout the world.

And it is not paradoxical in our peaceful efforts that we
maintain powerful military forces. For in a world partly
dominated by men who respect only guns, planes, and tanks,
these weapons are essential to our survival.

And let us remember this: war and peace, struggle and
resolution, hatred and concord are not merely the concerns
of government and diplomacy. They well up from the emotions and impulses in the hearts of individual men and
women, in every nation of the world.

These emotions, from generation to generation, are passed
on from parent to child. The problems these emotions create
are incredibly complex. Why must a country fight to the
death to hold seemingly worthless territory? Why must a
nation passionately strive to maintain an apparently meaning-

less boundary? Why must the people of one nation continue to hate or fear the people of another, for reasons lost in the dimness of the past?

Solution of these problems requires more than skillful diplomacy. Essential to lasting peace is a genuine desire of the individual citizens of each nation to understand the traditions and hopes and desires of the citizens of all other nations. We in America must strive to understand the emotions and attitudes, instilled in other peoples from childhood, which lie at the heart of vexing international difficulties. Above all we need the religious quality of compassion; the ability to feel the emotions of others as though they were our own. If the mothers in every land could teach their children to understand the homes and hopes of children in every other land—in America, in Europe, in the Near East, in Asia —the cause of peace in the world would indeed be nobly served.

But still more is essential to our cause than the capacity to understand the motivations which, ingrained in nations, divide them. We must probe through these to the more fundamental urgings, the bonds which make brothers of all men.

The desire to be free, the desire to realize one's own capacities, the desire for justice, the respect for reason, willingness to sacrifice for one's children, love of home, and love of peace—all these lie deep in the hearts of all peoples.

It must be so.

It is this Divinely inspired faith which gives promise to our quest for peace.

May this faith be ever nourished and strengthened in the families of America.

For these are the foundations, my friends, on which the men and women of our nation and of all nations which cherish freedom and peace can build an abiding happiness, for themselves, and for their children.

THE HOPE OF MANKIND

ADDRESS AT THE LIGHTING OF THE NATIONAL
COMMUNITY CHRISTMAS TREE
WASHINGTON, D.C., DECEMBER 17, 1954

Christmastide is a season of hope, of heartening hope for peace on earth, good will among men. This year, even as two thousand years ago, when the Prince of Peace was born into the world, the drums of war are stilled. In their silence, after a whole generation of almost ceaseless beating, many people already become fathers and mothers enjoy the first peaceful Christmas they have known. So, mankind's unquenchable hope for peace burns brighter than for many years.

Our hope, true enough, is blemished by some brutal facts.

Oppression, privation, cruel suffering of body and mind imposed on helpless victims, these scourges still wound in too many places the daily living of mankind.

Even at this happy season, we dare not forget crimes against justice, denial of mercy, violation of human dignity. To forget is to condone and to provoke new outrage.

Neither dare we forget our blessings. To count them is to gain new courage and new strength, a firmer patience under test and a stouter faith in the decency of man and in the providence of God.

Among the greatest of man's blessings this Christmas is his strengthened hope of lasting peace. But hope without works is the prelude to disillusionment. They, whose cause

Army Photographic Agency

PRESIDENT EISENHOWER BROADCASTS FROM THE WHITE HOUSE

is just, must be prepared to meet the harsh challenge of inertia; privation; despair; statism; materialism. This bright Christmas must not be followed by a Christmas of universal tragedy.

We Americans know that a mighty part of promoting and serving peace is ours to do.

With our friends, we must enlarge the design of our partnership so that we, who marched together in evil days when war and fear of war darkened the earth, shall enjoy together in days of light the rich rewards of a secure and stable era.

There are some who have believed it possible to hold themselves aloof from today's world-wide struggle between those who uphold government based upon human freedom and dignity, and those who consider man merely a pawn of the state. The times are so critical and the difference between these world systems so vital and vast that grave doubt is cast upon the validity of neutralistic argument. Yet we shall continue faithfully to demonstrate our complete respect for the right of self-decision by these neutrals. Moreover, because they hate aggression and condemn war for conquest, even as we, there is provided a strong foundation upon which we can proceed with them to build mutual understanding and sympathy.

Now, with those who stand against us, in fear or in ignorance of our intentions, we have chosen the hard way of patient, tireless search in every avenue that may lead to their better understanding of our peaceful purposes. They know, as well as we, that the world is large enough, the skills of man great enough, to feed and to clothe and to house mankind in plenty and in peace. This universal knowledge could be the fruitful beginning of a prosperous life together.

America speaks from strength—strength in good allies, in arms, in readiness, in ever-increasing productivity, in the broader sharing of the abundant fruits of our economy, in our unchanging devotion to liberty and to human justice. Her voice is for peace based upon decency and right. But let no man think that we want peace at any price; that we shall forsake principle in resigned tolerance of evident evil; or that we may pawn our honor for transitory concession.

At this Christmas season, America speaks too in humble gratitude for the friendship of peaceful peoples across the world. Without their warm confidence and faithful partnership, this earth would be a bleak ground of aimless and endless clash and conflict.

And America joins with all believers of every faith in a prayer of thanks and a plea that, whatever lies ahead, we may be strong and courageous and wise in the doing of our own task in accord with the Divine will.

To all the dwellers of the earth, I speak for this Republic, and directly from the heart of every one of its citizens, when I say that this nation prays for you—all of you—the fullness of the Christmas spirit, peace and good will.

And now, please permit me a personal note. My wife and I wish to all of you here, and to all peoples everywhere, a very merry Christmas. As I light the nation's Christmas tree, "God rest you . . . Let nothing you dismay."

(Here the President pressed the button that lit the tree)

And now, goodnight; and again, merry Christmas!

TWO GREAT GOALS

Always I feel it is a special privilege when I can meet with men and women of the newspaper profession. Our newspapers have traditionally been a guarantee that truth will reach every part of our own country and all the free peoples of the world. I have heard you referred to as a one-party press. If this is true, I do trust that the slogan, the purpose, the aim of your party is to spread the truth. If that is so, I apply for membership. Never was it more important than it is today that the people of the entire world have free access to the truth.

Recently I read a story about one particular segment of the newspaper community of America and how it helped spread the truth even beyond the barriers devised against its communication—into the homes of the Communist-dominated lands.

Some twenty thousand newspaper boys voluntarily conducted a fund-raising campaign for the Crusade for Freedom. That Crusade brings truth to those behind the Iron Curtain, to people who otherwise could not have it. Of course, the boys' campaign is not one of the normal functions of the American newspapers; but the incident gives heartening evidence of newspaper people's unflagging in-

43941

terest in the maintenance of freedom and of human hope for peace.

Certainly, I am inspired by the knowledge that boys of this nation will freely give of their time and their energy, and more important, their hearts, to help bring information of today's world to those whose masters provide them nothing but propaganda.

In this day, every resource of free men must be mustered if we are to remain free; every bit of our wit, our courage, and our dedication must be mobilized if we are to achieve genuine peace. There is no age nor group nor race that cannot somehow help.

Just over two years ago I had an opportunity to appear before the American Society of Newspaper Editors. I then pledged your Government to an untiring search for a just peace as a fixed and abiding objective. In our search for peace we are not bound by slavish adherence to precedent or halted by the lack of it. The spirit of this search influences every action of your Administration; it affects every solution to problems of the moment.

It prompted my proposal before the General Assembly of the United Nations that governments make joint contributions of fissionable materials to an International Atomic Energy Agency for peaceful research so that the miraculous inventiveness of man may be consecrated to his fuller life.

It inspired the offer of polio information, research facilities, and seed virus so that Dr. Salk's historic accomplishment may free all mankind from a physical scourge.

It provides the reason for a plan that, after lengthy study, I am able now to announce. We have added to the United States Program for Peaceful Uses of Atomic Energy an atomic-powered merchant ship. The Atomic Energy Commission and the Maritime Administration are now developing specifications. I shall shortly submit to the Congress a request for the necessary funds, together with a description of the vessel.

The new ship, powered with an atomic reactor, will not require refueling for scores of thousands of miles of operation. Visiting the ports of the world, it will demonstrate to people everywhere this peacetime use of atomic energy, harnessed for the improvement of human living. In part, also, the ship will be an atomic exhibit; carrying to all people practical knowledge of the usefulness of this new science in such fields as medicine, agriculture, and power production.

The search for peace likewise underlies the plan developed for expanding foreign trade embodied in a bill now before the Congress.

In every possible way, in word and in deed, we shall strive to bring to all men the truth of our assertion that we seek only a just and a lasting peace.

There is no precedent for the nature of the struggle of our time.

Every day, in our newspapers, we are confronted with what is probably the greatest paradox of history.

Out of an instinctive realization of the horror of nuclear war the hunger of virtually every human being on this planet is for tranquil security, for an opportunity to live and to let live, for freedom, for peace. And yet, defying this universal hunger, certain dictatorships have engaged in a deliberately conceived drive which periodically creates alarms and fears of war.

In our uneasy postwar world, crises are a recurrent international diet; their climaxes come and go. But so they have, in some degree, since the beginning of organized society. By their effect on human action, the peril within them is either magnified or diminished.

A crisis may be fatal when, by it, unstable men are stampeded into headlong panic. Then, bereft of common sense and wise judgment, they too hastily resort to armed force in the hope of crushing a threatening foe, although thereby they impoverish the world and may forfeit the hope for enduring peace.

But a crisis may likewise be deadly when inert men, unsure of themselves and their cause, are smothered in despair. Then, grasping at any straw of appeasement, they sell a thousand tomorrows for the pottage of a brief escape from reality.

But a crisis is also the sharpest goad to the creative energies of men, particularly when they recognize it as a challenge to their very resource, and move to meet it in faith, in thought, in courage. Then, greatly aroused—yet realizing that beyond the immediate danger lie vast horizons—they can act for today in the light of generations still to come.

The American people, one hundred sixty-four million of us, must recognize that the unprecedented crises of these days, packed with danger though they may be, are in fullest truth challenges that can be met and will be met to the lasting good of our country and to the world.

Two great American objectives are mountain peaks that tower above the foothills of lesser goals. One is global peace based on justice, mutual respect and co-operative partnership among the nations. The other is an expanding American economy whose benefits, widely shared among all our citizens, will make us even better able to co-operate with other friendly nations in their economic advancement and our common prosperity.

The fundamental hazard to the achievement of both objectives is the implacable enmity of godless communism. That hazard becomes the more fearsome as we are guilty of failure among ourselves; failure to seek out and face facts courageously; failure to make required sacrifices for the common good; failure to look beyond our selfish interests of the moment; failure to seek long-term betterment for all our citizens.

Recognizing the ruthless purposes of international communism, we must assure, above all else, our own national safety. At the same time we must continue to appeal to the sense of logic and decency of all peoples to work with us in the development of some kind of sane arrangement for peace.

But when a nation speaks alone, its appeal may fall on deaf ears. Many nations must combine their voices to penetrate walls of fear and prejudice, selfishness and ignorance.

The principal objective of our foreign policy, therefore, as we search for peace, is the construction of the strongest possible coalition among free nations. The coalition must possess spiritual, intellectual, material strength.

In things spiritual, the common effort must be inspired by fairness and justice, by national pride and self-respect. It must be based on the inalienable rights of the individual who—made in the image of his Creator—is endowed with a dignity and destiny immeasurable by the materialistic yard-stick of communism.

In things intellectual, the coalition must manifest such common sense and evident logic that all nations may see in it an opportunity to benefit themselves. Certainly, it must proclaim the right of all men to strive for their own betterment, and it must foster their exercise of that right.

In things material, the friendly partnership must be sin-ewed by expanded economies within all its member nations, mutually benefiting by a growing trade volume that must be joined in realization that their security interdependence is paralleled by their economic interdependence.

By sound economic thinking and action, we Americans can hasten the achievement of both our great goals: peace among the nations; a widely shared prosperity at home.

We have an unmatched production system. But even our economy will not thrive if confined to our own land. So to sustain our own prosperity and economic growth we must strengthen the economic bonds between us and others of the free world. Thus we confront the communist with a vast and voluntary partnership of vigorous, expanding national economies whose aggregate power and produc-tivity, always increasing, can never be successfully chal-lenged by the communist world.

The issue is clean-cut. Either we foster flourishing trade between the free nations or we weaken the free world and our own economy. Unless trade links these nations to-gether, our foreign policy will be encased in a sterile vac-uum; our domestic economy will shrink within its con-tinental fences. The enlargement of mutually beneficial trade in the free world is an objective to which all of us should be fully dedicated.

Ours is the most dynamic economy yet devised by man, a progress-sharing economy whose advance benefits every man, woman, and child living within it.

Last year, our Gross National Product exceeded 357 billion dollars. Twenty years ago few would have believed such an achievement even a remote possibility.

Nevertheless, continuation of current rates of increase will bring us by 1965 to 500 billion dollars or more as our Gross National Product. This will mean a tremendous advance in the living standards of the American people. But a 500 billion dollar economy by 1965 can be achieved only within the framework of a healthy and expanding free world economy.

Trade expands markets for the increased output of our mines, our farms, and our factories. In return we obtain essential raw materials and needed products of the farms and factories of others. Likewise, the markets provided here for the products of other free world countries enable them to acquire from us capital equipment and consumer goods essential to their economic development and higher living standards.

American agriculture sells abroad from one-fourth to one-third of major crops such as wheat, cotton, and tobacco. Without these export markets there can be, under current conditions, no enduring prosperity for the American farmer.

American factories and labor likewise have an important stake in foreign trade. Last year this country sold over 9 billion dollars of industrial products abroad. Over 3 million workers, American workers, are directly dependent on exports for their jobs. Jungles the world round are being tamed today by American bulldozers; new mines are being opened by our drills and equipment; fields that have been cultivated by hand for centuries are yielding new harvests to our agricultural machines; our automobiles, trucks, and buses are found wherever there are roads; and new industries to employ the teeming millions within the underdeveloped nations are being equipped with our machine tools.

The expansion of our foreign trade should proceed on an orderly basis. Reductions in tariffs and other trade barriers, both here and abroad, must be gradual, selective, and reciprocal. Changes which would result in the threat of serious injury to industry or general reduction in employment would not strengthen the economy of this country or the free world. The trade measures that I have recommended to the Congress were prepared in recognition of these facts.

Now, to abandon our program for the gradual reduction of unjustifiable trade barriers—to vitiate the Administration proposals by crippling amendments—would strike a severe blow at the co-operative efforts of the free nations to build up their economic and military defenses. It could result in increasing discrimination against our exports. It could lead to widespread trade restrictions and a sharp contraction in world trade. This would mean lowered production and employment at home. It could mean a retreat to economic nationalism and isolationism. It would constitute a serious setback to our hopes for global peace.

Two-way trade, I believe, is a broad avenue by which all men and all nations of good will can travel toward a golden age of peace and plenty. Your Administration is committed to help building it. I personally believe it is to the common good of all 164 million of our people and I shall not relax my personal effort towards its achievement.

We shall succeed, given the support of all who, unaffrighted by crises, are prepared to act on today's problems while they work for tomorrow's better and happier life. The accomplishment of this goal is worthy of the best effort of all Americans. Through you, the Press, and all your associates dedicated to the mission of spreading the truth, a more rapid progress can be made.

As we build a richer material world, we must always remember that there are spiritual truths which endure forever. They are the universal inspiration of all mankind. In them, men of both the free world and the communist world could well find guidance. Do we remember those words of our faith, "All things whatsoever ye would that men should do to you, do ye even so to them"?

Do we remind ourselves that a similar thread of peaceful and lofty exhortation reveals itself in the words of every one of the world's historic religious leaders? Every one of them, their followers today people great nations.

The Far East, the Middle East, the Near East, the West, Asia, and Africa, and Europe, and the American hemisphere all alike possess in their heritage the same universal ideal. Why then should we permit pessimism to slow our efforts; despair to darken our spirits?

Cannot we convince ourselves and others that in co-operation there is strength?

Cannot you, men and women of the pen, propagate knowledge of economic truth just as your professional forebears spread the truths that inspired our forefathers to achieve a national independence? For when all people, everywhere, understand that international trade, peaceful trade, is a fertile soil for the growth of a shared prosperity, of all kinds of co-operative strength, and of understanding and tolerance, the fruits thereof will be another historic step on the road to universal peace.

ANCIENT DREAM OF MAN

ADDRESS AT THE TENTH ANNIVERSARY MEETING OF

THE UNITED NATIONS

SAN FRANCISCO, CALIFORNIA, JUNE 20, 1955

This, my second appearance before the United Nations, gives me, as Chief Executive of the United States, the great privilege of joining with you in commemoration of an historic date, significant and momentous for all mankind.

I am privileged to bring you a special message from the Congress of the United States. Last week the Congress unanimously adopted a resolution requesting me to express to all of you here, on behalf of the people of the United States, our deep desire for peace and our hope that all nations will join with us in a renewed effort for peace.

Later this week my close friend and associate, Secretary John Foster Dulles, speaking with my full confidence and concurrence, will address you on appropriate elements in the foreign policy of the United States. Because of this circumstance, it seems fitting that I, today, speak principally in terms of my country's unswerving loyalty to the United Nations and of the reasons for our tireless support of it.

A decade ago, in this city, in this building, the Charter of the United Nations was signed by its fifty founding members. Into a world, shattered, and still at war, but hopeful and eager for a new dawn, was born an international organization, fashioned to be the supreme instrument of world peace.

For this nation, I pay respectful tribute to you whose faith, and patience, and courage, and wisdom have brought it through ten tumultuous, frequently discouraging, sometimes terrifying—but often rewarding years. That there have been failures in attempts to solve international difficulties by the principles of the Charter, none can deny. That there have been victories, only the willfully blind can fail to see. But clear it is that without the United Nations the failures would still have been written as failures into history. And, certainly, without this organization the victories could not have been achieved; instead, they might well have been recorded as human disasters. These, the world has been spared.

So, with the birthday congratulations I bring, I reaffirm to you the support of the Government of the United States in the purposes and aims of the United Nations, and in the hopes that inspired its founders.

Today, together, we face a second decade. We face it with the accumulated experience of the first ten years, as well as with the awful knowledge of nuclear weapons and the realization that a certain and enduring peace still eludes our persistent search.

But the summer of 1955, like that one of 1945, is another season of high hope for the world. There again stirs in the hearts of men a renewed devotion to the work for the elimination of war. Each of us here is witness that never in ten years has the will of many nations seemed so resolved to wage an honest and sustained campaign for a just and lasting peace. True, none of us can produce incontestable evidence to support this feeling. Nevertheless, all of us, I think, will testify that the heartfelt longings of countless millions for abundance and justice and peace seem to be commanding, everywhere, a response from their governments. These longings have strengthened the weak, encouraged the doubtful, heartened the tired, confirmed the believing. Almost it seems that men, with souls restored, are, with faith and courage, resuming the march toward the greatest human goal.

Within a month there will be a Four Power Conference of Heads of Government. Whether or not we shall then reach the initial decisions that will start dismantling the terrible apparatus of fear and mistrust and weapons erected since the end of World War II, I do not know.

The basis for success is simply put: it is that every individual at that meeting be loyal to the spirit of the United Nations and dedicated to the principles of its Charter.

I can solemnly pledge to you here, and to all the men and women of the world who may hear or read my words, that those who represent the United States, will strive to be thus loyal, thus dedicated. For us of the United States, there is no alternative, because our devotion to the United Nations Charter is the outgrowth of a faith deeply rooted in our cultural, political, spiritual traditions.

Woven into the Charter is the belief of its authors:

That man—a physical, intellectual, and spiritual being— has individual rights, divinely bestowed, limited only by the obligation to avoid infringement upon the equal rights of others;

That justice, decency, and liberty, in an orderly society, are concepts which have raised men above the beasts of the field: to deny any person the opportunity to live under their shelter is a crime against all humanity. Our Republic was born, grew, stands firm today in a similar belief.

The Charter assumes:

That every people has the inherent right to the kind of government under which it chooses to live and the right to select in full freedom the individuals who conduct that government.

Hence the Charter declares:

That on every nation in possession of foreign territories, there rests the responsibility to assist the peoples of those areas in the progressive development of free political institutions so that ultimately they can validly choose for themselves their permanent political status.

Our long history as a Republic manifests a self-imposed compulsion to practice these same principles.

The Charter recognizes that only those who enjoy free access to historical and current facts and information, and through objective education learn to comprehend their meanings, can successfully maintain and operate a system of self-government. Our Republic, likewise, maintains that access to knowledge and education is the right of all its citizens, and of all mankind.

Written under the shadow of war, the Charter is strong in the conviction that no nation has a right to employ force aggressively against any other. To do so, or to threaten to do so, is to defy every moral law that has guided man in his long journey from darkness toward the light. Those who wrote it clearly realized that global war has come to pose for civilization a threat of shattering destruction and a sodden existence by the survivors in a dark and broken world.

Likewise they recognized that the first responsibility of every nation is to provide for its own defense; and, in pursuance of this responsibility, it has the clear right to associate itself with other like-minded peoples for the promotion of their common security.

But they who wrote the Charter emphasized that in the formation of such associations, within the framework of the United Nations, it is incumbent upon the contracting parties to inform the world by solemn assurance, always supported by deeds, that the sole purpose is defense, devoid of aggressive aims.

We as a nation believe these truths that are expressed in the Charter. We strive to live by them. So, we shall always maintain a government at home that recognizes and constantly seeks to sustain for the individual those rich economic, intellectual, and spiritual opportunities to which his human rights entitle him.

In our relations with all other nations, our attitude will reflect full recognition of their sovereign and equal status. We shall deal with common problems in a spirit of partnership.

Insofar as our technical, material, and intellectual capacities permit and wherever our aid, including the peaceful use of atomic energy, may be needed and desired, we shall continue to help others achieve constantly rising economic levels. Thereby, we trust that they will have increased opportunity to attain their own cultural and spiritual aspirations.

We shall work with all others—especially through this great organization, the United Nations—so that peaceful and reasonable negotiations may replace the clash of the battlefield. In this way we can in time make unnecessary the vast armaments that, even when maintained only for security, still terrify the world with their devastating potentiality and tax unbearably the creative energies of men.

As some success in disarmament is achieved, we hope that each of the so-called great powers will contribute to the United Nations, for promoting the technical and economic progress of the less productive areas, a portion of the resultant savings in military expenditures.

An abiding faith inspired the men and women who devised the great Charter under which you work. We of the United States share that faith. We hold fast to the hope that all nations in their intercourse with others will observe those amenities of deportment, customs, and treatment of other nationals as are sanctioned by tradition, by logic, and by friendly purposes.

We and a majority of all nations, I believe, are united in another hope: that every government will abstain from itself attempting, or aiding others to attempt, the coercion, infiltration, or destruction of other governments in order to gain any political or material advantage, or because of differences in philosophies, religions, or ideologies.

We, with the rest of the world, know that a nation's vision of peace cannot be attained through any race in armaments. The munitions of peace are justice, honesty, mutual understanding, and respect for others.

So believing and so motivated, the United States will leave no stone unturned to work for peace. We shall reject no method however novel, that holds out any hope however faint, for a just and lasting peace.

May I recall to you the words of a great citizen of this country, Abraham Lincoln, which, though uttered in a different context, apply to the problem which the world now seeks to solve.

"The dogmas of the quiet past are inadequate to the stormy present. The occasion is piled high with difficulty, and we must rise with the occasion. As our case is new, so we must think anew and act anew. We must disenthrall ourselves, and then we shall save our country."

In such a body as this, it seems fitting that we should add to Lincoln's words: "Each for himself, our country and humanity."

The object of our second decade is still peace, but a peace of such a new kind that all the world will think anew and act anew.

It cannot be a mere stilling of the guns. It must be a glorious way of life. In that life the atom, dedicated once as man's slayer will become his most productive servant. It will be a peace to inspire confidence and faith so that all peoples will be released from the fear of war. Scientists will be liberated to work always for men, never against them. Who can doubt that in the next ten years world science can so beat down the ravages of disease and the pangs of poverty that humankind will experience a new expansion of living standards and of cultural and spiritual horizons. In this new kind of peace the artist, teacher, philosopher, workman, farmer, producer, and scientist will truly work together for the common welfare.

These hopes are not new. They are as old as history.

But now as we meet on this tenth anniversary in the city where was born the United Nations, we must realize that at last they are steadily and surely attainable. This is new. Our part—our part is to rededicate ourselves to the ideals of the United Nations Charter. May we here and now renew our determination to fulfill man's ancient dream, the dream which so inspired the founders of this organization.

Thus our duty will be nobly done, and future generations will behold the United Nations and stand up to call it blessed.

THE FORCE FOR PEACE

Within a matter of minutes I shall leave the United States on a trip that in some respects is unprecedented for a President of the United States. Other Presidents have left the continental limits of our country for the purpose of discharging their duties as Commander-in-Chief in time of war, or to participate in conference at the end of a war to provide for the measures that would bring about a peace. But now, for the first time, a President goes to engage in a conference with the heads of other governments in order to prevent wars, in order to see whether in this time of stress and strain we cannot devise measures that will keep from us this terrible scourge that afflicts mankind.

Now, manifestly, there are many difficulties in the way of a President going abroad for a period, particularly while the Congress is in session. He has many constitutional duties; he must be here to perform them. I am able to go on this trip only because of the generous co-operation of the political leaders in the Congress of both political parties who have arranged their work so that my absence for a period will not interfere with the business of the government. On my part I promised them that by a week from Sunday, on July 24th, I shall be back here ready to carry on my accustomed duties.

Now it is manifest that in such a period as I am able to spend abroad, we cannot settle the details of the many problems that afflict the world. But of course I go for a very serious purpose. This purpose is to attempt with my colleagues to change the spirit that has characterized the intergovernmental relationships of the world within the past ten years. Now, let us think for a moment about this purpose. Let us just enumerate a few of the problems that plague the world; the problem of armaments and the burdens that people are forced to carry because of the necessity for these armaments; the problem of the captive states, once a proud people that are now not allowed their own form of government freely chosen by themselves and under individuals freely elected by themselves; the problem of divided countries, people who are related to each other by blood and kinship but who are divided by force of arms into two camps that are indeed expected to be hostile to each other.

Then we have the problem of international interference in the internal affairs of free governments, bringing about a situation that leads to subversion, difficulties, and recriminations within countries, sometimes even revolutions.

These problems are made all the more serious by complications between governments. These problems of which I speak often have arisen as an aftermath of wars and conflicts. But governments are divided also by differing ambitions, by differing ideologies, by mutual distrust, and by the alarm that each creates. Because of these alarms, nations build up armaments and place their trust for peace and protection in those armaments. These armaments create greater alarms, and so we have a spiral of growing un-easiness and suspicion and distrust. That is the kind of thing that the world faces today. For these things there is no easy settlement. In the brief time that this conference can exist it is impossible to pursue all of the long and tedious negotiations that must take place before the details of these problems can be settled.

Our many postwar conferences have been characterized too much by attention to details, by an effort apparently to work on specific problems, rather than to establish a spirit and attitude in which to approach them. Success, therefore, has been meager. Too often, indeed, these con-ferences have been mere opportunities for exploitation of nationalistic ambitions, or, indeed, only sounding boards for the propaganda that the participants wanted to spread to the world.

If we look at this record we would say, "Why another conference? What hope is there for success?" Now, the first thing that I ask you is, "Do we want to do nothing; do we want to sit and drift along to the inevitable end of such a contest, to new tensions and then to war or at least to continuing tensions?"

We want peace. We cannot look at this whole situation without realizing, first, that pessimism never won any bat-tles, whether in peace or in war. Next, we will understand that one ingredient has been missing from all these con-ferences. I mean an intention to conciliate, to understand, to be tolerant, to try to see the other fellow's viewpoint as well as we see our own. I say to you, if we can change the spirit in which these conferences are conducted we will have taken the greatest step toward peace, toward future prosperity and tranquility that has ever been taken in the history of mankind.

I want to give you a few reasons for hope in this project: first, the people of all the world desire peace, that is, peace for people everywhere. I distinguish between people and governments here for the moment, for we know that the great hordes of men and women who make up the world do not want to go to the battlefield. They want to live in peace, not a peace that is a mere stilling of the guns, but a peace in which they can live happily, and in confidence that they can raise their children in a world of which they will be proud.

That common desire for peace is something that is a terrific force in this world and to which I believe all political leaders in the world are beginning to respond. They must recognize it.

Another item. Did you note this morning the speech made by Premier Bulganin in Moscow? Every word he said was along the lines that I am speaking. He talked of conciliation and tolerance and understanding. I say to you, I say to all the world, if the words that he expressed are as truly reflective of the hearts and minds of all the people in Russia, and the hearts and minds of all the people in all the world everywhere, there will be no trouble between the Russian delegation and our own at this coming conference.

Now I want to mention another item that is important in this conference. The free world is divided from the communist world by an iron curtain. The free world has one great factor in common. We are not held together by force but we are held together by this great factor.

It is this. The free world lives under one religion or another. It believes in a divine power. It believes in a supreme being. Now this, my friends, is a very great factor for conciliation and peace at this time. Each of these religions has as one of its basic commandments words that are similar to our Golden Rule, "Do unto others as you would have them do unto you." This means that the thinking of those people is based upon ideas of right, and justice, and mutual self-respect and consideration for the other man. This means peace, because only in peace can such conceptions as these prevail. This means that the free people of the world hate war; they want peace and are fully dedicated to it.

Now, this country, as other free countries, maintains arms. We maintain formations of war and all the modern weapons. Why? Because we must. As long as this spirit that has prevailed up to now continues to prevail in the world, we cannot expose our rights, our privileges, our homes, our wives, our children to the risk which would come to an unarmed country. But we want to make it perfectly clear that these armaments do not reflect the way we want to live. They merely reflect the way, under present conditions, we have to live. Now it is natural for a people steeped in a religious civilization, when they come to moments of great importance—maybe even crises such as now we face—to turn to the divine power that each has in his own heart, for guidance, for wisdom, for some help in doing the thing that is honorable, that is right.

I have no doubt that tonight throughout this country and indeed throughout the free world, that such prayers are ascending. This is a mighty force, and it brings to me the thought that through prayer we could also achieve a very definite and practical result at this very moment.

Suppose on the next sabbath day observed by each of our religions, Americans, 165 million of us, went to our accustomed places of worship, and, crowding those places, asked for help, and by so doing demonstrated to all the world the sincerity and depth of our aspirations for peace. This would be a mighty force. None could then say that we preserve armament because we want to. We preserve it because we must.

My friends, Secretary Dulles and I go to this conference in earnest hope that we may accurately represent your convictions, your beliefs, your aspirations. We shall be conciliatory because our country seeks no conquest, no property of others. We shall be tolerant because this nation does not seek to impose our way of life upon others. We shall be firm in the consciousness of your material and spiritual strength and your defense of your rights. But we shall extend the hand of friendship to all who will grasp it honestly and concede to us the same rights, the same understanding, the same freedom that we accord to them.

We, the Secretary and I, shall do our best with others there to start the world on the beginning of a new road, a road that may be long and difficult, but which, if faithfully followed, will lead us on to a better and fuller life.

FIRST STEPS TOWARD PEACE

STATEMENT AT THE GENEVA CONFERENCE

JULY 18, 1955

We meet here for a simple purpose. We have come to find a basis for accommodation which will make life safer and happier not only for the nations we represent but for people elsewhere.

We are here in response to a universal urge, recognized by Premier Bulganin in his speech of July 15, that the political leaders of our great countries find a path to peace.

We cannot expect here, in the few hours of a few days, to solve all the problems of all the world that need to be solved. Indeed, the four of us meeting here have no authority from others that could justify us even in attempting that. The roots of many of these problems are buried deep in wars, conflicts, and history. They are made even more difficult by the differences in governmental ideologies and ambitions. Manifestly it is out of the question in the short time available to the heads of government meeting here to trace out the causes and origins of these problems and to devise agreements that could with complete fairness to all, eliminate them.

Nevertheless, we can, perhaps, create a new spirit that will make possible future solutions of problems which are within our responsibilities. And equally important we can try to take here and now at Geneva the first steps on a new road to a just and durable peace.

The problems that concern us are not inherently insoluble. Of course, they are difficult; but their solution is not beyond the wisdom of man. They seem insoluble under conditions of fear, distrust, and even hostility, where every move is weighed in terms of whether it will help or weaken a potential enemy. If those conditions can be changed, then much can be done. Under such circumstances, I am confident that at a later stage our Foreign Ministers will be able to carry on from where we leave off, to find either by themselves or with others, solutions to our problems.

No doubt there are among our nations philosophical convictions which are in many respects irreconcilable. Nothing that we can say or do here will change that fact. However, it is not always necessary that people should think alike and believe alike before they can work together. The essential thing is that none should attempt by force or trickery to make his beliefs prevail and thus to impose his system on the unwilling.

The new approach we of this conference should seek cannot be found merely by talking in terms of abstractions and generalities. It is necessary that we talk frankly about the concrete problems which create tension between us and about the way to begin in solving them.

As a preface, may I indicate some of the issues I think we should discuss.

First is the problem of unifying Germany and forming an all-German government based on free elections. Ten years have passed since the German armistice, and Germany is still divided. That division does a grievous wrong to a people entitled, like any other, to pursue together a common destiny. While that division continues, it creates a basic source of instability in Europe. Our talk of peace has little meaning if at the same time we perpetuate conditions endangering the peace. Toward Germany, the four of us bear special responsibilities. While any conclusions we reach would be invalid unless supported by majority opinion in Germany, this problem should be a central topic for our meeting here. Must we not consider ways to solve it promptly and justly?

In the interest of enduring peace, our solution should take account of the legitimate security interests of all concerned. That is why we insist a united Germany is entitled at its choice, to exercise its inherent right of collective self-defense. By the same token, we are ready to take account of legitimate security interests of the Soviet Union. The Paris agreements contain many provisions which serve this purpose. But we are quite ready to consider further reciprocal safeguards which are reasonable and practical and compatible with the security of all concerned.

On a broader plane, there is the problem of respecting the right of people to choose the form of government under which they will live; and of restoring sovereign rights and self-government to those who have been deprived of them. The American people feel strongly that certain peoples of Eastern Europe, many with a long and proud record of national existence, have not yet been given the benefit of this pledge of our United Nations wartime declaration, reinforced by other wartime agreements.

There is the problem of communication and human contacts as among our peoples. We frankly fear the consequences of a situation where whole peoples are isolated from the outside world. The American people want to be friends with the Soviet people. There are no natural differences between our peoples or our nations. There are no territorial conflicts or commerical rivalries. Historically, our two countries have always been at peace. But friendly understanding between peoples does not readily develop when there are artificial barriers such as now interfere with communication. It is time that all curtains whether of guns or laws or regulations should begin to come down. But this can only be done in an atmosphere of mutual respect and confidence.

There is the problem of international communism. For thirty-eight years now, its activities have disturbed relations between other nations and the Soviet Union. Its activities are not confined to the efforts to persuade. It seeks throughout the world to subvert lawful governments and to subject nations to an alien domination. We cannot ignore the distrust created by the support of such activities. In my nation and elsewhere it adds to distrust and therefore to international tension.

Finally, there is the overriding problem of armament. This is at once a result and a cause of existing tension and distrust. Contrary to a basic purpose of the United Nations Charter, armaments now divert much of men's effort from creative to nonproductive uses. We would all like to end that. But apparently none dares to do so because of fear of attack.

Surprise attack has a capacity for destruction far beyond anything which man has yet known. So each of us deems it vital that there should be means to deter such attack. Perhaps, therefore, we should consider whether the problem of limitation of armament may not best be approached by seeking, as a first step, dependable ways to supervise and inspect military establishments, so that there can be no frightful surprises, whether by sudden attack or by secret violation of agreed restrictions. In this field nothing is more important than that we explore together the challenging and central problem of effective mutual inspection. Such a system is the foundation for real disarmament.

As we think of this problem of armament, we need to remember that the present burden of costly armaments not only deprives our own people of higher living standards, but it also denies the peoples of underdeveloped areas of resources which would improve their lot. These areas contain much of the world's population and many nations now emerging for the first time into political independence. They are grappling with the urgent problem of economic growth. Normally they would receive assistance particularly for capital development from the more developed nations of the world. However, that normal process is gravely retarded by the fact that the more developed industrial countries are dedicating so much of their productive effort to armament. Armament reduction would and should insure that part of the savings would flow into the less developed areas of the world to assist their economic development.

In addition, we must press forward in developing the use of atomic energy for constructive purposes. We regret that the Soviet Union has never accepted our proposal of December, 1953 that nations possessing stockpiles of fissionable material should join to contribute to a "world bank" so as, in steadily increasing measure, to substitute co-operation in human welfare for competition in means of human destruction. We still believe that if the Soviet Union would according to its ability contribute to this great project, the act would improve the international climate.

In this first statement of the Conference, I have indicated very briefly some of the problems that weigh upon my mind and upon the people of the United States, and where solution is largely within the competence of the four of us. As our work here progresses I hope that all of us will have suggestions as to how we might promote the search for the solution of these problems.

Perhaps it would be well if each of us would in turn give a similar indication of his country's views. Then we can quickly see the scope of the matters which it might be useful to discuss here and arrange our time accordingly.

Let me repeat. I trust that we are not here merely to catalogue our differences. We are not here to repeat the same dreary exercises that have characterized most of our negotiations of the past ten years. We are here in response to the peaceful aspirations of mankind to start the kind of discussions which will inject a new spirit into our diplomacy; and to launch fresh negotiations under conditions of good augury.

In that way, and perhaps only in that way, can our meeting, necessarily brief, serve to generate and put in motion the new forces needed to set us truly on the path to peace. For this I am sure all humanity will devoutly pray.

JUSTICE TO ALL NATIONS

Secretary Dulles and I, with our associates, went to the Big Four Conference at Geneva resolved to represent as accurately as we could the aspirations of the American people for peace and the principles upon which this country believes that peace should be based.

In this task we had the bi-partisan, indeed almost the unanimous, support of the Congress. This fact greatly strengthened our hand throughout the negotiations. Our grateful thanks go out to all your Senators and your Congressmen in the United States Congress. Aside from this, we had, during the past week, thousands of telegrams of encouragement and support from you as individuals. Along with these came similar telegrams from great organizations, church organizations, business and great labor organizations.

All of these combined served to make us feel that possibly we were faithfully representing the views that you would have us represent. Now peace, the pursuit of peace, involves many perplexing questions. For example:

Justice to all nations, great and small;

Freedom and security for all these nations;

The prosperity of their several economies and a rising standard of living in the world;

Finally, opportunity for all of us to live in peace and in security.

Now, naturally, in the study of such questions as these, we don't proceed recklessly. We must go prudently and cautiously, both in reaching conclusions and in subsequent action. We cannot afford to be negligent or complacent. But, we must be hopeful. We must have faith in ourselves and in the justice of our cause. If we don't do this, we will allow our own pessimism and our own lack of faith to defeat the noblest purposes that we can pursue.

Because of the vital significance of all these subjects, they will be exhaustively surveyed by our government over a period of many weeks. Tonight the most that I can give to you are a few personal impressions and opinions that may have some interest for you and certainly have some bearing on the outcome and on the progress of those negotiations.

Of course, an interesting subject that could be taken up, had I the time, would be the personalities of the several delegations, the relationship or apparent relationships of one to the other—the principal considerations that seem to motivate them. These would all have a bearing on this problem. But I forego them and take up instead just two general opinions in which I am sure every American shares.

The first of these, that we must never be deluded into believing that one week of friendly, even fruitful, negotiation can wholly eliminate a problem arising out of the wide gulf that separates, so far, East and West. A gulf as wide and deep as the difference between individual liberty and regimentation, as wide and deep as the gulf that lies between the concept of man made in the image of his God and the concept of man as a mere instrument of the State. Now, if we think of those things we are apt to be possibly discouraged.

But I was also profoundly impressed with the need for all of us to avoid discouragement merely because our own proposals, our own approaches, and our own beliefs are not always immediately accepted by the other side.

On the night I left for Geneva, I appeared before the television public to explain what we were seeking. I told you that we were going primarily to attempt to change the spirit in which these great negotiations and conferences were held. A transcript was made of that talk, and I should like now to read you one paragraph from it.

This is what I said with respect to our purpose: "We realize that one ingredient has been missing from all past conferences. This is an honest intent to conciliate, to understand, to be tolerant; to try to see the other fellow's viewpoint as well as we see our own. I say to you if we can change the spirit in which these conferences are conducted, we will have taken the greatest step toward peace, toward future prosperity and tranquility that has ever been taken in all the history of mankind."

During last week in formal conferences, and in personal visits, these purposes have been pursued. So now there exists a better understanding, a closer unity among the nations of NATO.

There seems to be a growing realization by all that nuclear warfare, pursued to the ultimate, could be practically race suicide.

There is a realization that negotiations can be conducted without propaganda and threats and invective.

Finally, there is a sharp realization by the world that the

United States will go to any length consistent with our concepts of decency and justice and right to attain peace. For this purpose, we will work co-operatively with the Soviets and any other people as long as there is sincerity of purpose and a genuine desire to go ahead.

In the course of carrying on these discussions there were a number of specific proposals, some of which were items on the official agenda. That agenda contained German reunification and European security, disarmament, and increased contacts of all kinds between the East and the West.

Most of these conference meetings were given wide publicity and even some of the specific suggestions made in those conferences likewise were publicized. In any event, I can assure you of one thing:

There were no secret agreements made, either understood agreements or written ones. Everything is put before you on the record.

Outside of these conference meetings there were numerous unofficial meetings; conversations with important members of the other delegations and, of course, specifically with the Soviet delegation.

In these conversations a number of subjects were discussed and among them the Secretary of State and I specifically brought up, more than once, American convictions and American beliefs and American concern about such questions as the satellites of Eastern Europe and the activities of international Communism. We made crystal clear what were American beliefs about such matters as these.

Now to take up for a moment the items on the official agenda.

Probably no question caused us as much trouble as that of

German reunification and European security. At first we thought that these could be dealt with separately, but the American delegation concluded that they had to be dealt with as one subject. We held that Germany should be reunited under a government freely chosen by themselves, and under conditions that would provide security both for nations of the East and for nations of the West, in fact in a framework that provided European security.

In the matter of disarmament, the American government believes that an effective disarmament system can be reached only if at its base there is an effective reciprocal inspection and overall supervision system, one in which we can have confidence and each side can know that the other side is carrying out his commitments. Because of this belief, we joined with the French and the British in making several proposals. Some were global, some were local, some were sort of budgetary in character. But all were in furtherance of this one single objective, that is, to make inspection the basis of disarmament proposals.

One proposal suggested aerial photography, as between the Soviets and ourselves by unarmed peaceful planes, and to make this inspection just as thorough as this kind of reconaissance can do. The principal purpose, of course, is to convince every one of Western sincerity in seeking peace. But another idea was this: if we could go ahead and establish this kind of an inspection as initiation of an inspection system we could possibly develop it into a broader one, and eventually build on it an effective and durable disarmament system.

In the matter of increasing contacts, many items were discussed. We talked about a freer flow of news across the curtains of all kinds. We talked about the circulation of books and particularly we talked about peaceful trade. But the subject that took most of our attention in this regard was the possibility of increased visits by the citizens of one country into the territory of another, doing this in such a way as to give each the fullest possible opportunity to learn about the people of the other nation. In this particular subject there was the greatest possible degree of agreement. As a matter of fact, it was agreement often repeated and enthusiastically supported by the words of the members of each side.

As a matter of fact, each side assured the other earnestly and often that it intended to pursue a new spirit of conciliation and co-operation in its contacts with the other. Now, of course, we are profoundly hopeful that these assurances will be faithfully carried out.

One evidence as to these assurances will, of course, be available soon in the language and the terminology in which we will find speeches and diplomatic exchanges couched. But the acid test should begin next October because then the next meeting occurs. It will be a meeting of the Foreign Ministers. Its principal purpose will be to take the conclusions of this conference as the subjects to be discussed there, and the general proceedings to be observed in translating those generalities that we talked about into actual specific agreements. Then is when real conciliation and some giving on each side will be definitely necessary.

For myself, I do not belittle the obstacles lying ahead on the road to a secure and just peace. By no means do I underestimate the long and exhausting work that will be necessary before real results are achieved. I do not blink the fact that all of us must continue to sacrifice for what we believe to be best for the safety of ourselves and for the preservation of the things in which we believe.

But I know that the people of the world want peace. Moreover, every individual at Geneva likewise felt this longing of mankind. So, there is great pressure to advance constructively, not merely to reenact the dreary performances, the negative performances of the past.

We, all of us, individually and as a people now have possibly the most difficult assignment of our nation's history. Likewise, we have the most shining opportunity ever possessed by Americans. May these truths inspire, never dismay us.

I believe that only with prayerful patience, intelligence, courage, and tolerance, never forgetting vigilance and prudence, can we keep alive the spark ignited at Geneva. But if we are successful in this, then we will make constantly brighter the lamp that will one day guide us to our goal—a just and lasting peace.

THE PRAYER BY WHICH WE LIVE

For hundreds of millions of us, Christmas symbolizes our deepest aspirations for peace and for goodwill among men.

For me, this particular Christmas has a very special meaning, and has brought to me, really, new understandings of people.

During the past three months my family and I have received literally thousands—tens of thousands of messages. Each of these has borne a sentence of good wishes and goodwill for health and happiness to us both. It has been heart-warming evidence that human understanding and human sympathy can surmount every obstacle; even those obstacles that some governments sometimes seem to raise in the attempt to divide us.

Now the free world is just coming to the close of a very significant year, one in which we have worked hard and sometimes effectively for peace. The facts of today, of course, do not measure up to the high hopes of the free world, the hopes by which we have lived and which we have long entertained. But this Christmas is, nevertheless, brighter in its background and its promise for the future than any we have known in recent years. I think it is even better than last year, and you will remember that Christmas was the first one in many years that was not marred by the tragic incidents of war.

Peace is the right of every human being. It is hungered for by all of the peoples of the earth. So we can be sure that tonight in the fullness of our hearts and in the spirit of the season, that as we utter a simple prayer for peace we will be joined by the multitudes of the earth.

Those multitudes will include rulers as well as the humblest citizens of lands; the great and the meek, the proud and the poor; the successful and the failures; the dispirited and the hopefuls.

Now each of those prayers will of course differ according to the characteristics and the personality of the individual uttering it, but running through every single one of those prayers will be a thought of this kind:

May each of us strive to do our best to bring about better understanding in the world. And may the infinite peace from Above live with us and be ours forever, and may we live in the confident hope that it will come.

And so it is tonight in that hope, which must never die from the earth, which we must cling to and cherish and nurture and work for, that I light the National Community Christmas Tree at the Pageant of Peace in Washington.

To each of you—wherever you may be—from Mrs. Eisenhower and me: a very Merry Christmas!

SEEKING WORLD SECURITY

ADDRESS AT THE ANNUAL DINNER OF THE
AMERICAN SOCIETY OF NEWSPAPER EDITORS
WASHINGTON, D.C., APRIL 21, 1956

When I last appeared before this body, almost exactly three years ago, stories from battlefields and fighting fronts crowded the front pages of our press. Human freedom was under direct assault in important sectors by the disciples of communistic dictatorship. Violence and aggression were brutal facts for millions of human beings. Fear of global war, of a nuclear holocaust, darkened the future. To many, the chance for a just and enduring peace seemed lost—hopeless.

Today, three years later, we have reason for cautious hope that a new, a fruitful, a peaceful era for mankind can emerge from a haunted decade. The world breathes a little more easily today.

Now the prudent man will not delude himself that his hope for peace guarantees the realization of peace. Even with genuine good will, time and effort will be needed to correct the injustices, to cure the dangerous sores that plague the earth today. And the future alone can show whether the Communists really want to move toward a just and stable peace.

Yet not for many years has there been such promise that patient, imaginative, enterprising effort could gradually be rewarded in steady decrease in the dread of war; in an economic surge that will raise the living standards of all the world; in growing confidence that liberty and justice will one day overcome statism; in the better understanding among all peoples that is the essential prelude to true peace.

This week marks the anniversary of one of the most important events in Freedom's progress. One hundred eighty one years ago on April 19th, our forefathers started a revolution that still goes on. The shots at Concord, as Emerson wrote, were heard "round the world." The echoes of Concord still stir men's minds.

The Bandung meeting, last year, of Asian and African leaders bears witness to Emerson's vision. There, almost two centuries after Concord, and halfway round the earth, President Sukarno of Indonesia opened the conference with an eloquent tribute to Paul Revere and to the spirit of the American Revolution.

Now why do the musket shots of a few embattled farmers at the Concord bridge still ring out in far-off lands?

The reason is clear. Concord was far more than a local uprising to redress immediate grievances. The enduring meaning of Concord lies in the ideas that inspired the historic stand there. Concord is the symbol of certain basic convictions about the relationship of man to the state.

These convictions were founded in a firm belief in the spiritual worth of the individual. He must be free to think, to speak, and to worship according to his conscience. He must enjoy equality before the law. He must have a fair chance to develop and use his talents. The purpose of government is to serve its citizens in freedom.

Our forefathers did not claim to have discovered novel

principles. They looked on their findings as universal values, the common property of all mankind.

These deep convictions have always guided us as a nation. They have taken deep root elsewhere in the Western world. In the 19th century they inspired a great surge of freedom throughout Western Europe and in our own hemisphere.

These ideas of freedom are still the truly revolutionary political principles abroad in the world. They appeal to the timeless aspirations of mankind. In some regions they flourish; in some they are officially outlawed. But everywhere, to some degree, they stir and inspire humanity.

The affairs of men do not stand still. The ideas of freedom will grow in vigor and influence, or they will gradually wither and die. If the area of freedom shrinks, the results for us will be tragic. Only if freedom continues to flourish will man realize the prosperity, the happiness, the enduring peace that he seeks.

II

The appeal of the ideas of freedom has been shown dramatically during the past decade. In that time, eighteen nations of 650 million people—almost a quarter of the population of the globe—have gained independence.

In manifold ways these nations differ widely from each other and from us. They are the heirs of many ancient cultures and national traditions. All of the great religions of the world are found among them. Their peoples speak in a hundred tongues.

Yet they share in common with all free countries the basic and universal values that inspired our nation's founders. They believe deeply in the right of self-government.

They believe deeply in the dignity of man. They aspire to improve the welfare of the individual, as a basis of organized society.

The new nations have many of the sensitivities that marked independence and are quick to resent any slight to their sovereignty. Some of them are concerned to avoid involvements with other nations, as we were for many long years.

Certainly we Americans should understand and respect these points of view. We must accept the right of each nation to choose its own path to the future.

All of these countries are faced with immense obstacles and difficulties. Freedom and human dignity must rest upon a satisfactory economic base. Yet in many of these new nations, incomes average less than $100 per year. Abject poverty blinds men's eyes to the beauty of freedom's ideals. Hopelessness makes men prey to any promise of a better existence, even the most false and spurious.

Oftimes the peoples of these countries expected independence itself to produce rapid material progress. Their political leaders are therefore under heavy pressure to find short-cuts and quick answers to the problems facing them.

Under these conditions, we cannot expect that the vision of a free society will go unchallenged. The Communists, aware of unsatisfied desires for better conditions of life, falsely pretend they can rapidly solve the problems of economic development and industrialization. They hold up the Soviet Union as a model and guide. But the Communists conceal the terrible human costs that characterize their ruthless system of dictatorship and forced labor.

Now we have a vital interest in assuring that newly independent nations preserve and consolidate the free institutions of their choice.

The prospects for peace are brightest when enlightened self-governing peoples control the policy of nations. People do not want war. Rulers beyond the reach of popular control are more likely to engage in reckless adventures and to raise the grim threat of war. So the spread of freedom enhances the prospect for durable peace.

That prospect would be dimmed or destroyed should freedom be forced into steady retreat. Then the remaining free societies, our own among them, would one day find themselves beleaguered and imperiled. We would face once again the dread prospect of paying dearly, in blood, for our own survival.

In every corner of the globe, it is far less costly to sustain freedom than to recover it when lost.

Moreover, our own well-being is bound up in the well-being of other free nations. We cannot prosper in peace if we are isolated from the rest of the world. If our economy is to continue to flourish and grow, our nation will need more trade, not less. The steady growth of other nations, especially the less developed nations, will create new and growing demands for goods and services. It will produce an environment which will benefit both them and us.

Indeed, Atlanta, Pittsburgh, Seattle—every American town and farm—has a stake in the success or failure of these new nations; a stake almost impossible to exaggerate.

If these new nations are to achieve economic progress with freedom, they will have to provide many of the necessary ingredients for themselves, indeed, most of them.

Only these peoples and their leaders can supply the initiative, the spark, and determination essential to success. And they must mobilize the larger part of the resources they require.

But these nations are gravely lacking in trained men for management, production, education, and the professions. Their institutions for such training are limited. Hence they are handicapped in trying to extend modern techniques to agriculture, industry, and other fields.

They also face shortages of capital and foreign exchange, even though they strain to mobilize their own resources. Private foreign investment should be utilized as much as feasible; but for many areas, it will clearly fall far short of the requirements. Moreover, their task of improving conditions of life is made the more difficult by their large and rapidly increasing populations.

Inevitably these nations must look abroad for assistance, as ours did for so many years. They want help, first of all, in real and understanding and enduring friendship. They want help in training skilled people and in securing investment capital to supplement their own resources. For such help they will look to us as the most prosperous and advanced economy of the world.

Foresight will compel an understanding response from us. In our own enlightened interest we can and must do much to help others in pursuit of their legitimate aspirations.

Further, we must recognize that economic and technical assistance cannot be a transitory policy. The problems of economic progress are not to be solved in a single spurt. Our efforts must be sustained over a number of years.

To do the most good, some part of our material help will have to be furnished on a long-term basis which these nations can plan on. For some purposes, commitments on a strictly annual basis are not sufficient. It takes time to complete major projects like hydroelectric and reclamation developments. If the new nations can plan on some part of our help for several years, they will be better able to mobilize resources of their own and assistance from others.

Furthermore, our assistance must be used flexibly to fit needs and plans as they develop. We must be ready to adapt our help promptly to meet changing conditions.

The development program for Mutual Security now before the Congress is based on these considerations. It seeks from the Congress the additional authority that would add essential flexibility and continuity to a part, a modest part, of the program. The amounts requested are the practicable minimum. In its entirety, it is not, I assure you, an excessive program. It is in our national interest, in the fullest sense of that term.

III

The ideas of freedom are at work, even where they are officially rejected. As we know, Lenin and his successors, true to Communist doctrine, based the Soviet State on the denial of these ideas. Yet the new Soviet rulers who took over three years ago have had to reckon with the force of these ideas, both at home and abroad.

The situation the new regime inherited from the dead Stalin apparently caused it to reappraise many of his mistakes.

Having lived under his one-man rule, they have espoused the concept of "collective" dictatorship. But dictatorship it still remains. They have denounced Stalin for some of the more flagrant excesses of his brutal rule. But the individual citizen still lacks the most elementary safeguards of a free society. The desire for a better life is still being sacrificed to the insatiable demands of the state.

In foreign affairs, the new regime has seemingly moderated the policy of violence and hostility which has caused the free nations to band together to defend their independence and liberties. For the present, at least, it relies more on political and economic means to spread its influence abroad. In the last year, it has embarked upon a campaign of lending and trade agreements directed especially toward the newly developing countries.

It is still too early to assess in any final way whether the Soviet regime wishes to provide a real basis for stable and enduring relations.

Despite the changes so far, much of Stalin's foreign policy remains unchanged. The major international issues which have troubled the postwar world are still unsolved. More basic changes in Soviet policy will have to take place before the free nations can afford to relax their vigilance.

IV

At Concord, our forebears undertook the struggle for freedom in this country. History has now called us to special tasks for sustaining and advancing this great cause in the world.

As we take stock of our position and of the problems that lie ahead, we must chart our course by three main guide lines:

The first one is: *We must maintain a collective shield against aggression to allow the free peoples to seek their valued goals in safety.*

We can take some cautious comfort in the signs that the Soviet rulers may have relegated military aggression to the background and adopted less violent methods to promote their aims. Nevertheless, Soviet military power continues to grow. Their forces are being rapidly modernized and equipped with nuclear weapons and long-range delivery systems.

So long as freedom is threatened and armaments are not controlled, it is essential for us to keep a strong military establishment ourselves and strengthen the bonds of collective security.

Without help from us, many of our allies could not afford to equip and maintain the forces needed for self-defense. Assistance to them is part of our proper contribution to the systems of common defense. If these systems did not exist, we would have to bear much greater costs ourselves. Thus in aiding our allies, the Mutual Security Program also advances our own security interests.

We hold our military strength only to guard against aggression, and to ensure that the world remains at peace. War in our time has become an anachronism. Whatever the case in the past, war in the future can serve no useful purpose. A war which became general, as any limited action might, could result in the virtual destruction of mankind.

Hence our search must be unceasing for a system to regulate and reduce armaments under reliable safeguards. So far, the Soviet Union has refused to accept such safeguards. But even now we are earnestly negotiating toward this end.

The problems involved are difficult and complex. We cannot afford to underestimate them. But we cannot afford to slacken our efforts to lift the burden of armaments and to remove their threat.

If effective measures of disarmament could be agreed upon, think how the world could be transformed! Atomic energy used for peace—not war—could bring about the development of a new industrial age. Far more human energy and output could be devoted to reducing poverty and need. To that end, as I said to this same body three years ago, we would "join with all nations in devoting a substantial percentage of the savings achieved from disarmament to a fund for world aid and construction."

Of even more importance, the pall of mutual suspicions, fear and hatred that covers the earth would be swept away in favor of confidence, prosperity, and human happiness.

Our second guide line is this: *Within the free community, we must be a helpful and considerate partner in creating conditions where freedom will flourish.*

Beyond defense, the crucial task of the free nations is to work together in constructive ways to advance the welfare of their peoples. Arms alone can give the world no permanent peace, no confident security. Arms are solely for defense, to protect from violent assault what we already have. They are only a costly insurance. They cannot add to human progress. Indeed, no matter how massive, arms by themselves would not prevent vital sections of the world falling prey to Communist blandishment or subversion.

If we are to preserve freedom here it must likewise thrive in other important areas of the earth. For the welfare of ourselves and others, we must, therefore, help the rest of the free world achieve its legitimate aspirations. For our mutual benefit, we must join in building for greater future prosperity, for more human liberty, and for lasting peace.

Within the Atlantic Community, our aim must be to strengthen the close bonds which have steadily developed since World War II.

In the less developed nations, the urgent need is for economic and social progress for their peoples. Tonight I have been speaking particularly about the newer nations of Asia and Africa, which face such urgent problems. Of equal importance is continuing progress in other areas, especially by our neighbors in Latin America who are our fast friends. These developing nations need the full measure of our help in understanding and resources.

The steady progress of the free world also depends on the healthy flow of peaceful trade. Our example will be of great importance in freeing the channels of such trade from wasteful restraints. We can take an important step to that end by joining the Organization for Trade Cooperation. Our national interest will be served by passage of the legislation for that purpose now pending in the Congress.

Another important task is in helping to resolve disputes between friends we value highly. Such disputes impair the unity of the free nations and impede their advance. In these situations, each side would like the United States to back its point of view without reservation. But for us to do so could seldom contribute to the settling of disputes. Rather, it would sharpen the bitter enmities between the opposing sides and impair our value in helping to reach a fair solution.

Our aim and effort must be to assist in tempering the fears and antagonisms which lead to such disputes.

My words apply with special force to the troubled area of the Middle East. We will do all in our power, through the United Nations whenever possible, to prevent resort to violence there in that region. We are determined to support and assist any nation in that area which might be subjected to aggression. We will strive untiringly to build the foundations for stable peace in the whole region.

In these and many other constructive ways, our nation must help to build an environment congenial to freedom.

Our third guide line is this: *We must seek, by every peaceful means, to induce the Soviet bloc to correct existing injustices and genuinely to pursue peaceful purposes in its relations with other nations.*

As I have said, many of the wrongs of Stalin against other nations still prevail under his successors. Despite the efforts of the West at Berlin and Geneva, Germany is still divided by the Soviet veto of free all-German elections. The satellite nations of Eastern Europe are still ruled by Soviet puppets. In Asia, Korea remains divided, and stable peace has not yet been achieved.

We must be tireless in our efforts to remedy these injustices and to resolve the disputes that divide the world. These knotty problems will eventually yield to patient and sincere effort. We stand ready to explore all avenues for their just settlement. We will not grow weary in our quest for peaceful remedies for the enslavement or wrongful division of once free nations.

The interests and purposes of the United States and of the free world do not conflict with the legitimate interests of the Russian nation or the aspirations of the Russian people. A Soviet government genuinely devoted to these purposes can have friendly relations with the United States and the free world for the asking. We will welcome that day.

V

My friends, we cannot doubt that the current world history flows toward freedom. In the long run dictatorship and despotism must give way. We can take courage from that sure knowledge.

But as a wise American, Mr. Justice Holmes, once said: "The inevitable comes to pass through effort." We should take these words to heart in our quest for peace and freedom. These great aspirations of humanity will be brought about, but only by devoted human effort.

Concord is a symbol of the faith, the courage, the sacrifice on which the victory of freedom depends. We in our day must strive with the same dedication that brought the militia men to the Concord bridge. If we do so, freedom will surely prevail.

After the President went off the air, he spoke extemporaneously to the Society:

To give you my feeling about what I would like to say now, I will tell you a story of when I was a young lieutenant in a regiment on the Mexican border. There was not a great deal to do in those days, and some people indulged in acquaintanceship with John Barleycorn more than they should.

One morning a couple of us young second lieutenants were up as usual long before the captains were, and we were standing by one captain's tent as he got his feet out of the bunk. He was sitting there on the edge of it with his head in his hands, and he says: "I am nothing but a mountain goat. All I do is jump from jag to jag."

Now any man who through thirty-five minutes or thirty minutes has been trying to hit the high spots of the world today, and America's position in the international situation, certainly feels that he has been jumping from jag to jag on the mountain tops.

So I wanted rather to come off the summit of those high spots and talk with you for just a few minutes about some of the very great intricacies in this problem we call developing foreign policies and in implementing them throughout the world.

Now I think there is no use explaining the cold war. We all have pretty clear ideas of what is going on. But one thing that we do worry about is: who is winning and who is losing?

Well, I don't think anybody knows, because the situation differs in every single corner of the globe. I have heard many people at home say that we are losing the cold war every day. Others take exactly the opposite view, and these more hopeful ones can point to some facts rather than merely allegations about our prestige abroad, or how many friends do we have, and that sort of thing.

For example, why was there such a sudden change in the Soviet policy? They are out—their basic aim is to conquer the world—through world revolution if possible, but in any way. Their doctrine, anyone that has read any of their books knows that their doctrine is lies, deceit, subversion, war if necessary, but in any way: conquer the world. And that has not changed.

But they changed their policies very markedly. They

were depending on force and the threat of force only. And suddenly they have gone into an entirely different attitude. They are going into the economic and political fields and are really wearing smiles around the world instead of some of the bitter faces to which we have become accustomed.

Now any time a policy is winning and the people are completely satisfied with it, you don't change. If you change policies that markedly, you destroy old idols, as they have been busy doing. You do it only when you think a great change is necessary. So I think we can take some comfort; at least we can give careful consideration to the very fact they had to change their policies.

And I think the whole free world is trying to test and determine the sincerity of that plan, in order that the free nations themselves, in pursuing their own policies, will make certain that they are not surprised in any place.

But from the Communists—we look at some of the advances we think they have made—but let us remember: they did not conquer Korea, which they announced they were going to do. They were stopped finally in the northern part of Vietnam, and Diem, the leader of the Southern Vietnam—the Southern Vietnamese, is doing splendidly and a much better figure in that field than anyone even dared to hope.

The Iranian situation which only a few short years ago looked so desperate that each morning we thought we would wake up and read in our newspapers that Mossadegh had led them under the Iron Curtain, has not become satisfactory, but that crisis has passed and it is much better.

The difficulty in Egypt between our British friends and our Egyptian friends over the big base was finally settled.

The Trieste problem which had plagued the world for many years, if not an ideal solution, has had a practical solution. The first bridgehead that Communism had succeeded, or practically succeeded in establishing in our hemisphere has been thrown out.

These are cold war victories, because the purposes of the Russians were defeated.

Now they have attempted to go into economic fields, and here their unity of action, brought about by the fact they are a single government, is creating new problems.

A group of free nations can stay together fairly easily when you have got a definite threat to their very existence right in their faces. As long as the Germans, for example, were powerful and aggressive in Europe in the Second World War, there was no great trouble in keeping the other nations pretty well together in policy and in action. But when those are lifted and you go into the economic field, each of us—each country—has its own economic problems of itself; now it becomes very difficult for a group of free nations through spontaneous co-operation to achieve a unity to oppose the other man.

Let me take one example just to show you how these things work out. Let us take Japan. There is no one who needs a blueprint of how important it is to us that Japan stay outside the Iron Curtain. A nation of ninety million industrious and inventive people, tied in with Communist China and with the Soviets, would indeed pose a threat to us that would be very grave indeed.

Japan is ninety million people living on fewer arable acres than there are in the State of California. How are they going to live? Well, they have got to trade. They have got to deal with other people outside. We won't trade with them. Every day—well, if not every day, every week—there comes to government, including to my desk, pleas for greater protection against Japanese goods.

Now this is not wholly one-sided, because some of our citizens have found out that last year—I think my figures are correct—while we were buying sixty million dollars' worth of cotton textile goods from Japan, they bought one hundred and twenty million dollars' worth of our cotton. So even that problem is not clear in exactly what you should do.

But anyway, we won't trade with them, so they can't make a living with us except on a minor scale. But we get tired. Properly, we can't be trying to sustain any other nation just with our money. So we don't just give them the millions by which they can go and buy all the things they need abroad.

But the next thing we come up against: we are very certain in our own minds that some of these nations—not all the United States people, but some of them—are very loud in their denunciation of any country that trades with the communist countries. So the Japanese can't trade with their natural markets, with Manchuria and China. So finally all of those southeastern markets—all the southeastern Asian markets have been largely destroyed—they are so poor they can't support Japan.

So what does Japan do? Where are we chasing her? Chasing her to one place. She has to look less and less to us and more to her mainland next to her. She has to, now, begin to look rather longingly, unless something is done. Now that is the kind of cross-purpose that comes up, and this goes on around the world. Britain and France and Germany, indeed every country with which we deal, has some problem different economically from our own.

So we have a real job in trying to get agreed policies among the free nations and then to implement them.

And I come, then, to the real purpose for asking you people to listen to me for a few minutes more after my rather long, prepared address.

It is this: Our nation is called to leadership—and I am not going to argue the point, I know you all understand—leadership in the world, to lead it towards freedom, to keep expanding our areas of freedom and not allow the communist cloud to engulf us little by little.

Now when a nation leads, it is not enough that even an entire government, legislative and executive, should see this problem as one. That doesn't make it a truly national policy in anything that is as long-term, as vital, as is required in national leadership of the whole world. Every citizen has a job that he cannot delegate. He cannot delegate it to the most powerful and the most influential political leaders. He must take his part in getting himself informed.

What I want to say is this: there is nothing more important in the world today than that America—167 million Americans—shall be informed on the basic facts in this whole struggle.

We ought to get it as far away from demagoguery, from political partisanship, from every extraneous influence as we possibly can. Just get the naked truth to these people with interpretation through editorial pages, and so on, to let them see the relation of one fact to another.

There are no easy panaceas. You can't say: "We simply

won't trade with the communist nations"—make that work for all of us. In fact, to make such a statement is, to my mind, giving up one of the great strengths for which the Yankee has always been noted: he is a good trader.

In that kind of trade, who gets the best of it?

We should think of those things and not try to pull out any slogan, any single idea, that will meet this situation. All that is necessary is to get the facts to the American people.

The other is to get, so far as we possibly can, the facts of America's purposes—her intentions, her disinterested motives, her lack of ambition for other territory and increased domination—to the world. We must get it out to the world.

This is difficult, because all over the world we don't have you people. We don't have American newspapers. Some of our wire services reach part way, but very inadequately. The United States Information Service is merely to help. It would be far better did we not have to depend on it at all. It should even itself depend on private media wherever it can reach them in other countries.

This information should go out abroad just as at home, through the processes of a free people so far as possible, and government should only support that effort.

One more point, and I am finished.

The world changes, and in these days it changes rapidly. A policy that was good six months ago is not necessarily now of any validity. It is necessary that we find better, more effective, ways of keeping ourselves in tune with the world's needs, and helping to educate the world to know that it itself—each nation—must do the major part of the job. Any outsider can merely be helpful, can give moral and some little physical support—material support.

But the sums that we put out are a bagatelle compared to what is needed and what these people, most of them impoverished, must provide for themselves if the whole free world is to advance.

Now there are different kinds of means: one of which, I should think, would be getting together and keeping a sort of rotating advisory body of citizens who are not burdened with the general and never-ending cares of office to devote their brains to the job in partnership with government. We must constantly keep "up to snuff" because if we don't, we are bound to lose. We must be ahead of the problem. We must see its major parts. We must get its critical factors set up so that we understand them thoroughly in simple fashion, and then we must pursue a common course vigorously, persistently, and with readiness to make whatever sacrifices may be demanded.

And then, I say, we will be worthy of the farmers of Concord.

FREEDOM IS THE DESTINY OF MAN

ADDRESS AT BAYLOR UNIVERSITY COMMENCEMENT CEREMONIES

WACO, TEXAS, MAY 25, 1956

This University is dedicated to true education; it strives to develop wisdom. This implies, over and beyond mere knowledge, an understanding of men's relationship to their fellow men in a world created for their stewardship by a God in whose image they are all made.

You have been taught here to do justice and to love mercy and to walk humbly before your Maker even as you use every opportunity to better yourselves through the profession in which you have been here grounded.

Now you enter a new phase of your life experience, in a world where the principles by which you live are frequently flouted and ignored. What is your place in this world? What can you do to improve it? Pointedly, what can each one of you as an individual do to promote a world society that respects the values in which you, and this school, believe so deeply. The thoughts I bring to you this morning deal primarily—and that most sketchily—with the international phases of a suggested answer.

I speak of international affairs for a very simple reason. In the fundamental struggle in which the world is now engaged, world issues create, or at least color, almost every domestic question, problem, and issue.

Clear comprehension of the basic factors involved is

vitally important to leaders and officials, indeed to every citizen of this country and of the world. Such understanding, I submit, is especially important to you young people who perforce must look at these critical current problems against a horizon of ten, twenty, forty years hence.

Today a militant, aggressive Communistic doctrine is dominant over much of the world's surface and over hundreds of millions of the world's people. In the postwar period, we have seen it indulge in a particularly cynical type of colonialism, expressed in the Communist subjugation of once free and proud nations in Europe and in Asia. Simultaneously, in the free areas of the world, six hundred million people in more than a score of new countries have achieved independence.

Communism denies the spiritual premises on which your education has been based. According to that doctrine, there is no God; there is no soul in man; there is no reward beyond the satisfaction of daily needs. Consequently, toward the human being, Communism is cruel, intolerant, materialistic. This doctrine, committed to conquest by lure, by intimidation and by force, seeks to destroy the political concepts and institutions that we hold to be dearer than life itself. Thus Communism poses a threat from which even this mighty nation is not wholly immune.

Yet, my friends, Communism is, in deepest sense, a gigantic failure.

Even in the countries it dominates, hundreds of millions who dwell there still cling to their religious faith; still are moved by aspirations for justice and freedom that cannot be answered merely by more steel or by bigger bombers; still seek a reward that is beyond money or place or power;

still dream of the day that they may walk fearlessly in the fullness of human freedom.

The destiny of man is freedom and justice under his Creator. Any ideology that denies this universal faith will ultimately perish or be recast. This is the first great truth that must underlie all our thinking, all our striving in this struggling world.

A second truth is that the fundamental principles of human liberty and free government are powerful sources of human energy, loyalty, and dedication. They are guides to enduring success. They are mightier than armaments and armies.

Americans have recognized those two truths in the historical documents of the Republic. They are repeated in the preamble to the fundamental policy statement in our current series of national security directives. In part that preamble reads:

> The spiritual, moral and material posture of the United States of America rests upon established principles which have been asserted and defended throughout the history of the Republic. The genius, strength and promise of America are founded in the dedication of its people and government to the dignity, equality and freedom of the human being under God.
>
> These concepts and our institutions which nourish and maintain them with justice are the bulwark of our free society and are the basis of the respect and leadership which have been accorded our nation by the peoples of the world.

Now, much as we are dedicated to this expression of lofty sentiment, it will count for little unless every American—to the extent of his influence and capacity—daily breathes into it the life of his own practice. The test is the readiness of individuals to cleave to principle even at the cost of narrower, more immediate gains.

For you graduates, and for all citizens, opportunities to strengthen our assault on injustice and bigotry will be as numerous as the tasks you undertake and the people that you meet each day. Nothing I might add could either quicken your recognition of such opportunities or strengthen your response to them. But certain it is that in this recognition and this response will be found the measure of America's future safety, progress, and greatness.

The third great truth that must underlie our thinking on international questions is this: People are what count. A sympathetic understanding of the aspirations, the hopes and fears, the traditions and prides of other peoples and nations, is essential to the promotion of mutual prosperity and peace. Such understanding is a compulsory requirement on each of us if, as a people, we are to discharge our inescapable national responsibility to lead the world in the growth of freedom and of human dignity.

Communism seeks to dominate or to destroy; freedom seeks to co-operate and to help others to build. But, my friends, these basic differences are not self-evident. Therefore, the people of the world are not necessarily thinking in terms of opposing concepts of communistic dictatorship and of human rights and freedom.

Rather, today, the most unyielding expression of peoples' aspirations seems to be an intense nationalism. There is nothing to be feared in this—of itself. The right of a people, capable of self-government, to their own political institutions is deeply imbedded in American thinking. Among peoples as among our own citizens we believe in the rights of the weak to be identical with those of the strong. And, in the past we have helped many small nations to independence. We will continue to hail with satisfaction the birth of each new nation whose people, achieving independence and freedom, become peaceful members of the world community.

In this day, however, one acute economic problem grows more acute as each new nation steps forward to an independent place in the international family. New nations, springing up, create new political boundaries. Far too often those political boundaries become serious obstacles to the flow of trade.

Such barriers are daily of more importance as increasing industrialization and specialization critically increase the economic interdependence of peoples. Specialization in any area—which implies an unbalanced local economy—is not necessarily a weakness, provided always that there is free opportunity for exchanging a portion of the products of such specialization for the other things needed to satisfy the requirements of all the people.

This means that, where any nation does not possess, within its own boundaries, the major elements of a broadly balanced economy, it is normally handicapped in assuring maximum satisfaction of human wants and prosperity for its own people. So we find that the emotional urge for a completely independent existence may seriously conflict with an equal desire for higher living standards.

This conflict, so obvious, is often ignored. But even the productivity and prosperity of this great country of ours would vanish if our States were forty-eight separate nations, with economic and political barriers at each boundary preventing or impeding the interflow of goods, people, and ideas.

We must put to ourselves this question: How can we help answer both the great desire of peoples for a separate, independent existence, and the need for economic union or, at least, effective economic co-operation among them.

This question is of vital importance to every nation. Unhappiness, unrest, and disaffection caused by depressed living standards can be as acute as when caused by political injustice. Disaffection, long continued, in any portion of the earth, can bring about political convulsions and grave global crises. In Communist areas the answer is achieved by compulsion.

But effective co-operation is not easily accomplished among free nations. Permit me in one illustration to point up the difficulty, among free peoples, of progress toward this type of union.

The statesmen of Western Europe have long been aware that only in broad and effective co-operation among the nations of that region can true security for all be found. They know that real unification of the separate countries there would make their combined two hundred and fifty million highly civilized people a mighty pillar of free strength in the modern world. A free United States of Europe would be strong in the skills of its people, adequately endowed with material resources, and rich in their common cultural and artistic heritage. It would be a highly prosperous community.

Without such unification the history of the past half century in Europe could go on in dreary repetition, possibly to the ultimate destruction of all the values those people them-selves hold most dear. With unification, a new sun of hope, security, and confidence would shine for Europe, for us, and for the free world.

Another stumbling block to European unity is the failure of populations as a whole to grasp the long-term political, economic, and security advantage of union. These are mat-ters that do not make for a soul-stirring address on a na-tional holiday. They can be approached only in thought, in wisdom—almost, I think we may say, in prayer.

Nevertheless—and happily—much progress has been made.

Years ago, our European partners began both to study and to act. Our country's help was given wherever possible be-cause our own future security and prosperity are inescapa-bly linked to those of our European friends. There was estab-lished the Brussels Compact, the Organization for European Economic Cooperation, the European Payments Union, the European Coal and Steel Community, and the Council for Europe. The North Atlantic Treaty Organization—NATO —although an organization comprehending much more than Western Europe, nevertheless provides the co-operative mechanism for greater security in the area. All these were set up to attack immediate problems in co-operation.

Despite setbacks and difficulties, these have been operating with increasing efficiency. So, European Union, one of the greatest dreams of Western man, seems nearer today than at any time in centuries, providing bright promise for the future of our European friends and for the growth and strength of liberty.

On a broader geographical scale, members of the Atlantic

Community are working together in many different ways and through many different agencies. But such co-operation can usefully be further developed. At the NATO meeting several weeks ago it was decided that the members of the Atlantic Community should "examine actively further measures which might be taken at this time to advance more effectively their common interests." They designated a Committee of three Foreign Ministers to advise on "ways and means to improve and extend cooperation in non-military fields and to develop greater unity within the Atlantic Community."

This effort recognizes the truth that all peoples of the free world must learn to work together more effectively in the solution of our common problems or the battle for human liberty cannot be won. Among equals, attempting to perform a difficult task, there is no substitute for co-operation.

It is gratifying, to all of us, I know, to realize that Senator Walter George has agreed to act as my Personal Representative and Special Ambassador in working for this new evolution of the Atlantic Community. Nothing could testify more forcefully to the critical importance of this project than the willingness of Senator George to undertake it.

Patiently but persistently we must work on. We must take into account man's hunger for freedom and for food; all men's dignity as well as some men's power; the eventual triumph of right and justice over expediency and force.

The responsibility for carrying forward America's part in helping improve international co-operation cannot be met through paper work in a governmental bureau. But it can be met through a combined effort by all of us, in and out

of government, all trying to develop the necessary understanding that every international problem is in reality a human one. You—the fortunate graduates of this great institution—are in a particularly advantageous position to lead in
the development of this kind of thinking and understanding.

You owe it to yourselves, you owe it to your country to
continue your study and critical analysis of the great international questions of our day. You can join with like-minded
men and women in the many voluntary associations that
promote people-to-people contact around the world. By
means of them, the thorny problems of the time are scruti-
nized from many viewpoints. Solutions are approached by
many avenues. Creative thinking is sparked. Mutual understanding is furthered.

Thus, every thinking person will come to understand that
his country's future will be brighter as the lot of mankind
improves; that no nation can in the long run prosper except
as the world enjoys a growing prosperity.

We must indeed be partners for peace and freedom and
prosperity, if those words are to record achievement as well
as to express a dream.

The foreign policy of this Republic—if it serves the enduring purposes and good of the United States—must always
be founded on these truths, thus expressing the enlightened
interests of the whole American people.

Certainly the basic foreign relations measures taken by the
United States in this century have been so developed. They
do not belong to any political party—they are American.
These measures range from our support of the Organization
of American States to our membership in the United Nations
and our present programs of partnership and assistance.

The United Nations by its very comprehensiveness is a unique association within which nations of every political complexion and philosophy have their place. The smaller groupings, in which we hold membership, are bound together by a common respect for common values. They conform, of course, to the United Nations Charter. But in each organization the likeness in background or interest or purpose that characterizes the membership and the restricted geographical limits within which it operates assures more effective discharge of their functions than is possible in a group as large as the United Nations.

We shall continue in our loyalty to the United Nations. But we should, at the same time, further expand and strengthen our other international associations.

Some of them, although only a few years old, are already household words, recognized as immense contributions to the prosperity and security of particular areas in the free world, and to our own prosperity and security. Yet none provides a complete answer to any of our international problems. Again, consider NATO.

A united Western Europe may still be on the far-off horizon. NATO is nevertheless a great alliance, rich in human and natural resources. But this great array is neither self-sustaining nor self-sufficient. Its freedom and prosperity and security are intertwined with the freedom and prosperity and security of many other nations—old and new and still to be born—that people an even greater portion of the earth. Within this community of freedom, all are more sure of their independence and prosperity and security when all of us join so that, first:

Mutual trade is fostered.

Legitimate political and economic aspirations are advanced.

Cultural traditions are respected.

The difficulties and misfortunes of the weaker are met by help from the stronger. To be backward, or penny wise in our practice of this truth can lead only to greater risk and greater cost—far greater cost to ourselves.

The ways in which progress along these four roads can be achieved are legion in number. The first, of which I've spoken at some length, is the need for the growth and spread of understanding among our own people. The next need is that the peoples of other nations must, through similar study and thought, recognize with us the need for this kind of co-operation. This is not easy. Many nations, though their cultures are ancient and rich in human values, do not possess the resources to spread the needed education throughout their populations. But they can wisely use help that respects their traditions and ways.

For example, the whole free world would be stronger if there existed adequate institutions of modern techniques and sciences in areas of the world where the hunger for knowledge and the ability to use knowledge are unsatisfied because educational facilities are often not equal to the need.

Do we not find here a worthy challenge to America's universities and to their graduates? I firmly believe that if some or all of our great universities, strongly supported by private foundations that exist in number throughout this land, sparked by the zeal and fire of educated Americans, would devote themselves to this task, the prospects for a peaceful and prosperous world would be mightily enhanced.

I honestly believe that the opportunity here for each

educated American is invaluable beyond the comprehension, almost, of any one of us.

In no respect should the purpose of these institutions be to transplant into new areas the attitudes, the forms, the procedures of America. The staffing, the conduct, the curriculum of each school would be the responsibility of the people where the school might be built.

Each school would help each nation develop its human and natural resources, and also provide a great two-way avenue of communication.

Such a voluntary effort in people-to-people partnership would be a dynamic, a fruitful corollary to three elements already effectively at work in our governmental foreign policy. For example:

To our Atoms for Peace program.

To our efforts to establish a climate in which universal disarmament can go forward.

To our long-sustained campaign for the exchange of knowledge and factual information between peoples.

Purposes and projects such as these—formulated by Republicans and Democrats—are part of a comprehensive effort to meet present and future needs, to solve problems in the enlightened self-interest of the United States.

It is not a haphazard, makeshift arrangement to meet day-to-day crises—big or little or imaginary.

Instead, it is a platform for the development of a stable, prosperous, peaceful world. Immediately concerned with this year and next year, our foreign policy is a realistic approach to a better world for all in 1966, 1976, 1996.

The basic objectives I have described are in furtherance of the aspirations of those who founded this Republic. These objectives are plainly advanced if we foster and secure conditions at home and abroad with which this system of freedom can live and under which it can find fertile ground for acceptance and growth. Thus our security and our aspirations are linked with the security and aspirations of liberty loving people in many other lands. It is idle to talk of community of interest with them in measures for defense, without recognizing community of interest with them in that which is to be defended.

So today it is vitally important that we and others detect and pursue the ways in which cultural and economic assistance will mean more to free world strength, stability, and solidarity than will purely military measures.

You of this class, like all Americans, must act in terms of today. At the same time, you in particular should think in terms of those years that now seem so distant.

You have in your heritage the dynamic principles that arouse visions in mankind.

You have in your hearts and minds the means to lift the eyes of men and women above the drab and desolate horizon of hate and fear and hopelessness.

My friends of Baylor—as Texans, as Americans—you believe in the brotherhood of man, and in his right to freedom. You are joined with millions of dedicated men and women at home, and linked in partnership with hundreds of millions of like-minded people around the globe. So believing and so united, you constitute the mightiest temporal force for good on this globe of ours.

A DEDICATION TO BROTHERHOOD

To address a thought to the heads of the American States here assembled is indeed a unique opportunity and a unique honor. I profoundly appreciate it.

We here commemorate the most successfully sustained adventure in international community living that the world has seen. In spite of inescapable human errors in our long record, the Organization of American States is a model in the practice of brotherhood among nations. Our co-operation has been fruitful because all of our peoples hold certain spiritual convictions. We believe:

That all men are created equal;

That all men are endowed by their Creator with certain inalienable rights, including the right to life, liberty, and the pursuit of happiness;

That government is the creation of man, to serve him, not to enslave him;

That those who demonstrate the capacity for self-government thereby win the right to self-government;

That sovereign states shall be free from foreign interference in the orderly development of their internal affairs.

Now, inspired by our faith in these convictions, our nations have developed in this hemisphere institutional relations and a rule of international law to protect the practice of that faith.

Our association began as we experienced the solemn but glorious transition from colonialism to national independence. Our association was intensified as we sought to maintain that independence against recurrent efforts of colonial powers to reassert their rule. More recently it has been perfected to protect against encroachments from the latter day despotisms abroad.

We are pledged to one another by the Inter-American Treaty of Reciprocal Assistance of 1947 to treat an armed attack by any State against an American State as an attack against all of us. We are joined in the 1954 Declaration of Solidarity for the Preservation of the Political Integrity of the American States against international Communist Intervention.

Furthermore, we are organized to assure peace among ourselves. The time is past, we earnestly believe, when any of our members would use force to resolve hemispheric disputes. Our solemn promises to each other foresee that the community will take whatever measures may be needed to preserve peace within America.

In all of these matters, our nations act as sovereign equals. Never will peace and security be sought at the price of subjecting any nation to coercion or interference in its internal affairs.

Thus, much has been done to assure the kind of national life which was the lofty vision of those early patriots who, in each of our countries, founded our Republics and foresaw the values inherent in hemispheric co-operation.

And so we reach today. May it not be that we can now

look forward to a new phase of association, in which we shall dedicate to individual human welfare the same measure of noble effort that heretofore has protected and invigorated the corporate life of our nations?

I do not suggest that the initial task is ended. A nation's peace and liberty can never be taken for granted. We must constantly be vigilant, individually and collectively. But we can, I believe, in the coming years, consecrate more effort to enriching the material, intellectual and spiritual welfare of the individual.

Since the day of creation, the fondest hopes of men and women have been to pass on to their children something better than they themselves enjoyed. That hope represents a spark of the Divine which is implanted in every human breast.

Too often, from the beginning, those hopes have been frustrated and replaced by bitterness or apathy.

Of course, the problems thus presented are primarily those of the particular country in which the affected individuals reside. But I believe we can be helpful to each other. The possibilities of our partnership are not exhausted by concentration in the political field. Indeed our Organization has already begun to apply the principle that material welfare and progress of each member is vital to the well-being of every other. But we can, I think, do more.

On this matter a simple thought which I have had an opportunity to express to some other American Presidents here has been viewed generously by them. It is that each of us, as President of an American Republic, should name a special representative to join in preparing for us concrete recommendations for making our Organization of American

States a more effective instrument in those fields of co-operative effort that affect the welfare of the individual. To those
representatives of ours we could look for practical suggestions in the economic, financial, social, and technical fields
which our Organization might appropriately adopt. As one
useful avenue of effort they could give early thought to
ways in which we could hasten the beneficial use of nuclear
forces throughout the hemisphere, both in industry and in
combatting disease.

So earnestly, my friends, do I believe in the possibilities
of such an organization for benefiting all our people, that
in my own case and with the agreement of the other Presidents to this Organization, I shall ask my brother, Milton
Eisenhower, already known to nearly all the Presidents here,
to be my representative on such an organization. He would,
of course, in the necessary cases, be supported by the professional and technical men whose assistance would be required.

Now, the coming years will bring to mankind limitless
ways in which this nuclear science can advance human welfare. Let us progress together, as one family, in achieving for
our peoples these results.

Our Organization can never be static. We are here to
commemorate a dynamic concept initiated at the first Inter-
American Conference of 1826 convoked by Simon Bolivar.
We here pay tribute to the faith of our fathers, which was
translated into new institutions and new works. But we cannot go on forever merely on the momentum of their faith.
We, too, must have our faith and see that it is translated into
works. So, just as our nations have agreed that we should
join to combat armed aggression, let us also join to find the

ways which will enable our peoples to combat the ravages of disease, poverty, and ignorance. Let us give them, as individuals, a better opportunity not only to pursue happiness, but to gain it.

A great family history has drawn together this unprecedented assemblage of the Presidents of the Americas. Perhaps, in our day, it may be given us to help usher in a new era which will add worthily to that history. Thus, we too will have served the future, as we have been greatly served by the past that we honor here today.

WE MUST PROCEED BY FAITH

In this Nation's capital city we are joined tonight with millions in all our forty-eight States, and, indeed, throughout the world, in the happiness and in the hope that Christmas brings.

Not that everyone is filled with happiness and hope in this season of rejoicing. Far from it. There is weariness, there is suffering for multitudes. There is hunger as well as happiness, slavery as well as freedom in the world tonight. But in the myriads of Christmas candles we see the vision of a better world for all people.

In the light of Christmas, the dark curtains of the world are drawn aside for the moment. We see more clearly our neighbors next door; and our neighbors in other nations. We see ourselves and the responsibilities that belong to us. Inspired by the story of Christmas we seek to give of our happiness and abundance to others less fortunate. Even now the American people, on the farm and in the city, rallying through the Red Cross and other voluntary agencies to meet the needs of our neighbors in Hungary, are true to the spirit of Christmas.

Even more important, there are particularly manifested during this season those spiritual qualities of freedom and

PRESIDENT AND MRS. EISENHOWER AND THEIR FAMILY ON
THE PORTICO OF THE WHITE HOUSE, CHRISTMAS, 1958

honor and neighborliness and good will—great virtues that make all peoples one. Through them, and faith in them, we see how men can live together in peace; for one glorious moment we sense progress toward that aspiration of every religious faith—"Peace on earth, good will to men."

These are hallowed words; through ages they have heartened and moved mankind, even though their message of peace is far too often drowned by the strident voices of the fearful or the arrogant who fill our minds with doubt and pessimism. They blur our vision with clouds of hate.

But the spirit of Christmas returns, yet again, to enable us to gain understanding of each other; to help each other; to obey the elemental precepts of justice; to practice good will toward all men of every tongue and color and creed; to remember that we are all identical in our aspirations for a peaceful, a decent, a rewarding life.

In the warm glow of the Christmas tree, it is easy to say these things, but when the trees come down and the lights are put away, as they always are, then we have a true testing of the spirit. That testing will be answered, throughout the year ahead, by the success each of us experiences in keeping alive the inspiration and exaltation of this moment.

We must proceed by faith, knowing the light of Christmas is eternal, though we cannot always see it.

We must believe that the truth of Christmas is constant; that men can live together in peace as Lincoln said, "with charity for all, with firmness in the right."

In this spirit, I now turn on the lights of the National Christmas Tree.

By the light of Christmas charity and Christmas truth, we enter the New Year with gratitude and strength. In this spirit, let us make sure that 1957 will add a memorable chapter to the story of mankind.

Now, on behalf of Mrs. Eisenhower and myself, may I wish for all of you in this audience—throughout our nation—throughout the world—a truly Merry Christmas. And may the Father of us all bless all who dwell upon the earth.

THAT MAN MAY WALK UNAFRAID

As once again we meet in this annual ceremony, we count ourselves a very fortunate people. In a land at peace, we are gathered about the National Christmas Tree to set its lights aglow with their symbolic message of peace and good will to men.

The custom we now observe brings us together for a few minutes on this one night. But this brief ceremony is warm in a spirit that gives meaning to all our days and all our labors.

For you and I, here, are not alone in a world indifferent and cold. We are part of a numerous company—united in the brotherhood of Christmas. And, as a brotherhood, we remember with special concern, the weak, the helpless, the hungry.

And beyond this tree that towers above us in the dusk; beyond the shadows and limits of this place, a mighty host of men and women and children are one great family in the spirit of Christmastide.

Tens of millions of them are fellow Americans. At this moment they are sitting in safe and cheerful homes. They visit among themselves in the lighted squares of small towns. They hurry along the crowded streets of busy cities. Freely they drive and fly and ride the transport lanes of the nation. They are at work, at work of their own choosing, in shops and factories and fields. They are on distant posts and stations, and on the approaches to the South Pole and to Greenland, on every continent and on many islands, doing their tasks far from home for the peace and well-being of all of us at home.

All are united in the renewed hope which we feel at Christmas time, that the world will somehow be a better place for all of us.

In the days just preceding our Holiday Season, I had the opportunity to work closely with the leaders of our NATO allies. Later this evening, the Secretary of State and I shall report to America on that meeting. But here let me say that, in dedication to peace, in our determination and readiness collectively to sustain that peace, we are firmly joined with our NATO partners—as indeed we are with other friendly nations around the world.

And, across national boundaries, and the mountains and oceans of the earth, hundreds of millions more are one with us. They speak in many tongues. They walk by many paths. They worship through many rites and, in some lands, observe different Holy Days. But by the good cheer they spread, the fellowship they express, the prayers that each makes to his own Heaven—they are all akin and like to us.

The spirit of Christmas helps bridge any differences among us. Faith and hope and charity are its universal countersigns. Peace and good will are its universal message. But these noble words will be words only, hollow and empty, unless we confirm them:

In sweat and toil that translate good intentions into fruit-ful action;

In courage that does not hesitate because the risk is great or the odds immeasurable;

In patience that does not quit because the road is hard or the goal far off;

In self-sacrifice that does not dodge a heavy duty because the cost is high or the reward unsure.

And so we confirm our faith that men may walk one day unafraid under the Christmas light, at peace with themselves and their fellows.

To all peoples who prize liberty, who seek justice and peace for their fellowmen, even to those who in the climate of this era may fear or suspect us, I speak for all Americans in a heartfelt message that happiness may belong to all men at this Christmastide.

Now, as I turn on the lights of our National Christmas Tree, Mrs. Eisenhower joins me in the wish to all of you, our fellow countrymen, that God will keep and bless you and give you a Merry Christmas.

TO RESIST AGGRESSION

Mr. Chairman, I must assure you that our audience here will be aware of a great deal of duplication in our two speeches. It does not dismay me, though, to repeat these sentiments, for the simple reason that one of the reasons that I am here is to assure you of the identity of view on the part of the American people to those that have just been so well expressed.

It is with a sense of high distinction that I accepted the invitation to address you. I deem this a great personal honor, and a bright symbol of the genuine friendship between the peoples you and I represent.

I bring to this nation of four hundred million, assurance from my own people that they feel that the welfare of America is bound up with the welfare of India. America shares with India the deep desire to live in freedom, human dignity, and peace with justice.

A new and great opportunity for that sort of life has been opened up to all men by the startling achievements of men of science during recent decades. The issue placed squarely before us today is the purpose for which we use science.

Before us we see long years of what can be a new era; mankind in each year reaping a richer harvest from the fields of earth . . . gaining a more sure mastery of elemental power for human benefit . . . sharing an expanding commerce in goods and in knowledge and in wisdom . . . dwelling together in peace.

But history portrays a world too often tragically divided by misgiving and mistrust and quarrel. Time and again governments have abused the fields of earth by staining them with blood and scarring them with the weapons of war. They have used a scientific mastery over nature to win a dominance over others . . . even made commerce an instrument of exploitation.

The most heartening, hopeful phenomenon in the world today is that people have experienced a great awakening. They see the evils of the past as crimes against the moral law, injuring the offender as well as the victim. They recognize that only under the rule of moral law can all of us realize our deepest and noblest aspirations.

One blunt question I put to you, and to all—everyone— everywhere who like myself share responsibility assigned to us by our people:

Must we continue to live with prejudices, practices, and policies that will condemn our children and our children's children to live helplessly in the pattern of the past, awaiting possibly a time of war-borne obliteration?

We all fervently pray not. Indeed, there can be no statesmanship in any person of responsibility who does not concur in this world-wide prayer.

Over most of the earth, men and women are determined that the conference table shall replace the propaganda mill; international exchange of knowledge shall succeed the international trade in threats and accusations; and the fertile

works of peace shall supplant the frenzied race in armaments of war.

Our hope is that we are moving into a better era. For
my part, I shall do all I can, as one human working with
other humans, to push toward peace; toward freedom; toward dignity and a worthy future for every man and
woman and child in the world.

If we—and especially all those occupying positions of
responsibility—give all that is within us to this cause, the
generations that follow us will call us blessed. Should we
shirk the tasks or pursue the ways of war—now become
ways to annihilation and race suicide—there may be no
generations to follow us.

I come here representing a nation that wants not an acre
of another people's land; that seeks no control of another
people's government; that pursues no program of expansion in commerce or politics or power of any sort at another people's expense. It is a nation ready to co-operate toward achievement of mankind's deep, eternal aspirations
for peace and freedom.

And I come here as a friend of India, speaking for one
hundred and eighty million friends of India. In fulfilling
a desire of many years, I pay in person America's tribute to
the Indian people, to their culture, to their progress, and
to their strength among the independent nations.

All humanity is in debt to this land. But we Americans
have, with you, a special community of interest.

You and we from our first days have sought, by national
policy, the expansion of democracy. You and we, peopled
by many strains and races speaking many tongues, wor-
shipping in many ways, have each achieved national

strength out of diversity. And you and we, never boast that ours is the only way. We are conscious of our weaknesses and our failings. We both seek the improvement and betterment of all our citizens by assuring that the state will serve, not master, its own people or any other people.

Above all, our basic goals are the same.

Ten years ago, your distinguished Prime Minister, when I was his host at Columbia University in New York, said:

"Political subjection, racial inequality, economic misery—these are the evils we have to remove if we would assure peace."

Our Republic, since its founding, has been committed to a relentless, ceaseless fight against those same three evils: political subjection, racial inequality, economic misery.

Not always has America enjoyed instant success in a particular attack on them. By no means has victory been won over them and, indeed, complete victory can never be won so long as human nature is not transformed. But in my country, through almost two hundred years, our most revered leaders have been those who have exhorted us to give of our lives and our fortunes to the vanquishment of these evils. And in this effort for the good of all our people, we shall not tire nor cease.

Ten years have passed since Mr. Nehru spoke his words. The pessimist might say that, not only do the three evils still infest the world—entrenched, and manifold; but that they will never lose their virulence. And the future, he might conclude, will be a repetition of the past; the world stumbling from crisis in one place to crisis in another; given no respite from anxiety and tension; forever fearful that inevitably some aggression will blaze into global war.

Thus might the pessimist speak. And were we to examine only the record of failure and frustration, we all would be compelled to agree with him.

We Americans have known anxiety and suffering and tragedy, even in the decade just past. Tens of thousands of our families paid a heavy price that the United Nations and the rule of law might be sustained in the Republic of Korea. In millions of our homes there has been, in each, the vacant chair of absent men—a son who performing his duty gave some of the years of his youth that successful aggression might not come to pass. The news, from near and distant places, that has reached us in America through these ten years, has been marked by a long series of harsh alarms.

These alarms invariably had their source in the aggressive intentions of an alien philosophy backed by great military strength. Faced with this fact, we in America have felt it necessary to make clear our own determination to resist aggression through the provision of adequate armed forces. These forces serve us and those of our friends and allies who like us have perceived the danger. But they so serve for defensive purposes only. In producing this strength, we believe we have made a necessary contribution to a stable peace, for the present and for the future as well.

Historically and by instinct, the United States has always repudiated and still repudiates the settlement, by force, of international issues and quarrels. Though we will do our best to provide for free world security, we continue to urge the reduction of armaments on the basis of effective reciprocal verification.

And contrasting with some of our disappointments of the

past decade, and the negative purposes of security establishments, Americans have participated, also, in triumphant
works of world progress, political, technical, and material.
We believe these works support the concept of the dignity
and freedom of man. These hearten America that the years
ahead will be marked by like and greater works. And
America watches, with friendly concern, the valiant efforts
of other nations for a better life, particularly those who
have newly achieved their independence.

Ten years ago India had just achieved independence;
wealthy in courage and determination, but beset with problems of a scale and depth and numbers scarcely paralleled
in modern history. Not even the most optimistic of on-
lookers would then have predicted the success you have
enjoyed.

Today, India speaks to the other nations of the world
with greatness of conviction and is heard with greatness of
respect. The near conclusion of her second five-year program is proof that the difficulty of a problem is only the
measure of its challenge to men and women of determined
will. India is a triumph that offsets the world's failures of
the past decade; a triumph that, as men read our history a
century from now, may offset them all.

India has paced and spurred and inspired men on other
continents. Let anyone take a map of the earth and place
on it a flag wherever political subjection has ended, racial
prejudice has been reduced, economic misery at least partially relieved, during the past ten years, he will find evidence in the cluster of these flags that the ten years past
may well have been the ten most fruitful years in the age-
old fight against the three evils.

Because of these ten years, today our feet are set on the road leading to a better life for all men.

What blocks us that we do not move forward instantly into an era of plenty and peace?

The answer is obvious: We have not yet solved the problem of fear among the nations. The consequence is that not one government can exploit the resources of its own territory solely for the good of its people.

Governments are burdened with sterile expenditures . . . preoccupied with the attainment of a defensive military posture that grows less meaningful against today's weapons carriers.

Much of the world is trapped in the same vicious circle. Weakness in arms often invites aggression or subversion, or externally manipulated revolutions. Fear inspired in others by the increasing military strength of one nation spurs them to concentrate still more of their resources on weapons and war-like measures. The arms race becomes more universal. Doubt as to the true purpose of these weapons intensifies tension. Peoples are robbed of opportunity for their own peaceful development. The hunger for a peace of justice and good will inevitably becomes more intense.

Controlled, universal disarmament is the imperative of our time. The demand for it by the hundreds of millions whose chief concern is the long future of themselves and their children will, I hope, become so universal and so insistent that no man, no government anywhere, can withstand it.

My nation is committed to a ceaseless search for ways through which genuine disarmament can be reached. And my government, even as I said more than six years ago, in

April of 1953, still . . . "is ready to ask its people to join with all nations in devoting a substantial percentage of the savings achieved by disarmament to a fund for world aid and reconstruction."

But armaments of themselves do not cause wars—wars are caused by men.

And men are influenced by a fixation on the past, the dead past, with all its abuses of power; its misuses of responsibility; all its futile convictions that force can solve any problem.

In the name of humanity, can we not join in a five-year or a fifty-year plan against mistrust and misgiving and fixations on the wrongs of the past? Can we not apply ourselves to the removal or reduction of the causes of tension that exist in the world? All these are the creations of governments, cherished and nourished by governments. The peoples of the world would never feel them if they were given freedom from propaganda and pressure.

Permit me to cite two simple examples from my own experience. As President of the United States, I welcomed into our Union last year a new sovereign State, Hawaii. Peopled by all the races of the earth, men and women of that new State having their ancestral homes in Asia and Africa and Europe, the two Americas, and the islands of the earth. Those peoples are of every creed and color, yet they live together in neighborly friendliness, in mutual trust, and each can achieve his own good by helping achieve the good of all.

Hawaii cries insistently to a divided world that all our differences of race and origin are less than the grand and indestructible unity of our common brotherhood. The world should take time to listen with attentive ear to Hawaii.

As President of Columbia University, every year we welcomed to its campus, students from every continent, from almost every nation that flew a flag, and some from tribes and colonies not yet free. In particular there still lives in my memory, because of their eagerness and enthusiasm for learning, the presence of hundreds of young people from India and China and Japan and the other Asian countries that studied among us, detached from any mutual prejudice or any fixation over past wrongs, indeed, these vices are not easily discernible among the young of any people.

These two simple things from my own experience convince me that much of the world's fear, suspicion, prejudice, can be obliterated. Men and women everywhere need only to lift up their eyes to the heights that can be achieved together; and, ignoring what has been, push together for what can be.

Not one wrong of years ago that still rankles; not one problem that confronts us today; not one transitory profit that might be taken from another's weakness, should distract us from the pursuit of a goal that dwarfs every problem and wrong of the past.

We have the strength and the means and the knowledge. May God inspire us to strive for the world-wide will and the wisdom that are now our first needs.

In this great crusade, from the history of your own nation, I know India will ever be a leader.

A SINGLE RULE OF LAW

REMARKS DELIVERED AT UNIVERSITY OF NEW DELHI

NEW DELHI, INDIA, DECEMBER 11, 1959

Among the honors which are bestowed upon men in public life, few awards have the dignity and symbolic importance which attach to an honorary degree granted by a world-renowned university. Realizing this fact, with the deepest gratitude and humility, I am proud to accept—in the name of the American people, Mr. Chancellor—this token of spiritual brotherhood.

Universities in the modern world have a difficult dual function to perform. They must be at the same time strong-holds of traditional wisdom accumulated during the ages and alert outposts of a world advancing toward the conquest of the unknown. Within them, the traditional and the new are continually being molded together to form the substance of a better life for humans.

We are fortunate in the United States that we have had the opportunity to draw deeply from the wells of ancient enlightenment in other cultures. The treasures of Indian philosophical thought and writing have not been alien to the intellectual development of America.

In the last twenty years, our long-established interest in Indian studies has increased in scope and in intensity. And now, American scholars are seriously concerning themselves with the economic problems, the politics, and the social structure of your great experiment in democracy.

This scholarly effort reflects the growing conviction in my country that no nation can or should live by itself, isolated from the life-giving streams of other cultures.

I have been glad to learn that American studies are being introduced into the curriculum of this splendid University and in other outstanding universities in India.

I know, too, that thousands of your young men and women are studying in American schools, and that hundreds of our professors have come to India to learn from a country whose rich history goes back thousands of years.

Through this exchange of thoughtful people, this trading of ideas and of ideals, this patient building of a bridge of mutual understanding, we accelerate our march toward the goal of world peace.

History teaches us two lessons that are pertinent to the role of a university in this march.

The first is: Mutual good is ever the product of mutual understanding.

The second is: A world of swift economic transformation and growth must also be a world of law.

As to the first, the need for great mutual understanding among the peoples, what has been done in the exchange of students should be only a beginning. These young people are a vital, dynamic element in the world's resources for the construction of a just and secure peace.

Most of us who have been given responsibility by our people have reached years of maturity. In some cases, prejudices and antagonisms we have acquired are so much a part of ourselves that they are not easy to eradicate. The older we grow the more stubbornly we cling to conceptions, and misconceptions, that have long been with us in response to real or fancied wrongs.

On the other hand, all of us recognize the ease with which young people absorb new ideas, new insight. I urge then that we amplify our thinking about the security and the peace of the world to embrace the role of our young people.

I propose to you that, while Governments discuss a meeting of a few at the summit, universities consider a massive interchange of mutual understanding on the grand plateau of youth.

More enduringly than from the deliberations of high councils, I believe mankind will profit when the young men and women of all nations, and in great numbers, study and learn together. In so doing, they will concern themselves with the problems, the possibilities, the resources and the rewards of a common destiny.

Through centuries nations have sent their youth, armed for war, to oppose their neighbors. Let us, in this day, look on our youth, eager for larger and clearer knowledge, as forces for international understanding; and send them, one nation to the other, on missions of peace.

On the second lesson of history:

The time has come for mankind to make the rule of law in international affairs as normal as it is now in domestic affairs. Of course, the structure of such law must be patiently built, stone by stone. The cost will be a great deal of hard work, both in and out of Government—particularly in the universities of the world.

Plainly one foundation stone of this structure is the International Court of Justice. It is heartening to note that a strong movement is afoot in many parts of the world to increase acceptance of the obligatory jurisdiction of that Court. And I most heartily congratulate India on the leadership and vision she has shown in her new declaration accepting the jurisdiction of that Court.

Another major stone in the structure of international rule of law must be a body of international law adapted to the changing needs of today's world. There are dozens of countries which have attained their independence since the bulk of existing international law was evolved. What is now needed is to infuse into international law the finest traditions of all the great legal systems of the world. And here the universities of the world can be of tremendous help in gathering and sifting and harmonizing them into universal law.

Universities and research centers, in my own country, are now beginning specific projects aimed at tapping the deepest wellsprings of major legal systems, as well as the most modern developments of law around the globe.

A reliable framework of law, grounded in the general principles recognized by civilized nations, is of crucial importance in all plans for rapid economic development around the earth. Economic progress has always been accompanied by a reliable legal framework. Law is not a concrete pillbox in which the status quo is armed and entrenched. On the contrary, a single rule of law, the sanctity of contract, has been the vehicle for more explosive and extensive economic change in the world than any other single factor.

One final thought on rule of law between nations: We will all have to remind ourselves that under this system of law one will sometimes lose as well as win. But here is another thought: Nations can endure and accept an adverse decision, rendered by competent and impartial tribunals.

This is so, I believe, for one good reason: If an international controversy leads to armed conflict, everyone loses; there is no winner. If armed conflict is avoided, therefore, everyone wins. It is better to lose a point now and then in an international tribunal, and gain a world in which everyone lives at peace under a rule of law.

Here then are two purposes which I see as particularly fitting within the mission of the world's universities:

A more massive mobilization of young people in the centers of learning where truth and wisdom are enshrined and ignorance and witless prejudice are corrected. They whose world this soon will be, can thus begin to make it now a more decent place for their living.

Second, an inquiry and a search into the laws of the nations for the grand principles of justice and righteousness and good, common to all peoples; out of them will be constructed a system of law, welcome to all peoples because it will mean for the world a rule of law—and end to the suicidal strife of war.

In purusing these purposes, the universities—I most firmly believe—will add new glory to their names for they will be giving leadership to the worthiest human enterprise—the pursuit of peace with justice.

I repeat, that I am proud to accept this University's degree—on behalf of the American people.

UNDER ONE BANNER

I am signally honored by the invitation to join President Prasad at the opening of the World Agriculture Fair—the first such Fair as this ever held. And it is entirely right that it be held here in India. For this Nation recognizes in agriculture the fundamental occupation of man and the chief assurance of better living for its citizens.

My own country was quick to accept when invited to participate in this historic event. And today I am particularly honored that India's Chief of State will be with me when, in a few minutes, I officially open the United States Exhibit at the Fair. Indeed, the occasion of this Fair gave me the very finest reason I could think of to make this the time of the visit to India that I had long determined upon.

At this American Exhibit, all visitors can see how we Americans have managed the soil of our land so that our people might live well for themselves; and have enough food left over to help others. Our way is not necessarily the best, even for us, but here we depict in the American Exhibit, American agriculture as it is. We do have a natural pride in what we have accomplished by a creative union of human spirit, fertile earth, and inventive science. But, beyond this, we see in modern agriculture a most effective instrument for a better life among all men. *Mela USA* points up its use for that high purpose.

On the personal side, I visit this Fair with keen interest. As a boy and young man, I grew up in the heart of the American farmland. A long-held ambition during my professional years, not always too well concealed, has been to return to the farm. And I plan to be a farmer when my present form of occupation comes to a close. So, I have a keen interest in spending a bit of time at this Fair where so many nations present their achievements in methods and techniques and ways of agriculture. I shall see here much that is new to me. Many of these things are probably improvements on what I have seen or done in the past, and I hope I am still not too old to learn.

For a moment, I hope you will indulge me as I suggest some thoughts on how food can help all of us achieve better lives in a world of justice and peace.

Today, we have the scientific capacity to abolish from the world at least this one evil, we can eliminate the hunger that emaciates the bodies of children; that scars the souls of their parents; that stirs the passions of those who toil endlessly and earn only scraps.

Men, right now, possess the knowledge and the resources for a successful world-wide war against hunger—the sort of war that dignifies and exalts human beings. The different exhibits in this whole Fair are clear proof of that statement.

The call to that genuinely noble war is enunciated in the theme of the American Exhibit:

"Food–Family–Friendship–Freedom."

Into these four words are compressed the daily needs, the high purposes, the deep feelings, the ageless aspirations that unite Indians and Americans under one banner—the banner of human dignity.

Here are four words that are mightier than arms and bombs; mightier than machines and money; mightier than any empire that ruled the past or threatens the future.

Here are four words that can lift the souls of men to a high plane of mutual effort, sustained effort, the most rewarding effort that can be proposed to mankind.

First Food: food that our bodies may be fit for every task and duty and service; our minds free from the fear of hunger; our eyes, undimmed by the tragedies of famine, searching out new horizons; our aspirations not frustrated by failure of crop or catastrophe of weather.

Family: family that in our homes there may be decent living and bright hope; children, no longer doomed to misery in peace and sudden death in war; their elders, no longer broken by want and sorrow beyond their control to mend or cure.

Friendship: that among all the peoples of earth the darkness of ignorance and fear and distrust will dissolve in the light of knowledge and understanding. The time has come when we must all live together for our mutual betterment or we shall all suffer harsh, possibly the final, penalty.

Freedom: that on all continents and islands of the earth every man and woman of good will and good life may make the proudest of human boasts: "I am free; slave to no tyranny imposed by other men, by the accident of birth, by the whims of circumstance."

The American Exhibit at this Fair presents the role we feel agriculture can play in furtherance of a healthy, fruitful, peaceful world where the families of all nations can live in freedom from fear of famine and war.

In no wise whatsoever is the American Exhibit an attempt to portray our agriculture as superior to any other. Through centuries of living with the soil and streams, the environment and climate of their own lands, people have learned adjustments and adaptations peculiarly suited to their own circumstances.

What we do present here are ways in which American farmers multiplied their productivity; the fertility of their fields; the vigor and the value of their livestock.

In this Exhibit visitors will see the techniques, the changes in old methods, the applications of new discoveries that have best served America's particular requirements. Modified to fit your needs and your circumstances, it is our hope that they might be of value to you.

Of course, they cannot work miracles overnight, in any land. But with each harvest, they may help to bring every people using them closer to a dependable self-sufficiency.

Early this year, I set in motion a new program "to explore anew with other surplus-producing nations all practical means of utilizing the various agricultural surpluses of each in the interest of reinforcing peace and the well-being of free peoples throughout the world—in short, using food for peace."

In keeping with this program my government and the government of India have been working together. Whatever strengthens India, my people are convinced, strengthens us, a sister-Republic dedicated to peace. This great nation of four hundred million people, rich in culture and history, courageous in the resolve to be free and strong, is a mighty influence for an enduring and just peace in the world. And this is true of every nation so courageous, so determined, so inspired as is India.

With them we shall continue to co-operate to achieve a world free from the pangs of hunger, in which families live full and prosperous lives, where friendship among nations replaces fear and suspicion, and where men are free in the pursuit of happiness.

THE HELP WE MUST GIVE

Fellow Americans, at home and overseas; Friends of America; Workers for a just peace wherever you may be in the world, whatever your race or flag or tongue or creed:

Once again I have the privilege of lighting the Pageant of Peace Tree on the eve of the Christmas season. This is the season when men and women of all faiths, pausing to listen, gain new heart from the message that filled the heavens over Bethlehem two thousand years ago: "Peace on earth—Good will to men."

Every Christmas through the long march of centuries since then, the message has been echoed in the hopes and prayers of humanity.

This Christmas, for me at least those words have clearer meaning, sharper significance, more urgent counsel.

Last night I came home from a trip that carried me to three continents, Africa and Asia and Europe. I visited eleven countries whose populations total a quarter of all mankind.

I wish that every American—certainly every American recognized by his fellows as a leader in any field, and every leader in the countries of the West—could see and hear what I have seen and what I have heard. The mutual understanding thereby created could in itself do much to dissolve the issues that plague the world.

My trip was not undertaken as a feature of normal diplomatic procedures. It was not my purpose either to seek specific agreements or to urge new treaty relationships. My purpose was to improve the climate in which diplomacy might work more successfully; a diplomacy that seeks, as its basic objective, peace with justice for all men.

In the crowds that welcomed my party and me, I saw at close hand the faces of millions. Many, indeed most, were poor, weary, worn by toil, but others were young, energetic, eager; the children, as always, bright and excited.

The clothes of a few were as modern as today's Paris and New York; of others, as ancient as the garb of Abraham; often soiled and tattered; although sometimes colorful and romantic to the American eye.

They were Buddhist and Moslem and Hindu and Christian.

But seeing them massed along country roads and city streets from the Eastern shore of the Atlantic to Karachi and Delhi, three things—it seemed to me—united them into one family.

The first: Their friendship for America and Americans.

The second: Their fervent hope, too long frustrated, for betterment of themselves and of their children.

And third: Their deep-seated hunger for peace and freedom.

Of this last, permit me to speak first. It must come first. The assurance of peace in freedom is the key to betterment of peoples everywhere; and in a just peace friendship between all peoples will flourish.

I assure you that all the people I saw and visited want

peace—nothing in human affairs can be more certain than that.

I talked with Kings and Presidents, Prime Ministers and humble men and women in cottages and in mud huts. Their common denominator was their faith that America will help lead the way toward a just peace.

They believe that we look and work toward the day when the use of force to achieve political or commercial objectives will disappear; when each country can freely draw on the culture, wisdom, experience of other countries and adapt to its own needs and aspirations what it deems is best and most suitable.

They understand that we look and work toward the day when there can be open and peaceful partnership, communication, interchange of goods and ideas between all peoples; toward the day when each people will make its maximum contribution toward the progress and prosperity of the world.

Such is the world condition which we and all the peoples I visited hope—and pray—to see.

Our concept of the good life for humanity does not require an inevitable conflict between peoples and systems in which one must triumph over the other. Nor does it offer merely a bare coexistence as a satisfactory state for mankind.

After all, an uneasy coexistence could be as barren and sterile, joyless and stale a life for human beings as the coexistence of cellmates in a penitentiary or a labor camp.

We believe that history, the record of human living, is a great and broad stream into which should pour the richness and diversity of many cultures; from which emerge ideas and practices, ideals and purposes, valid for all.

We believe each people of the human family, even the least in number and the most primitive, can contribute something to a developing world embracing all peoples, enhancing the good of all peoples.

But we recognize—we must recognize—that in the often fierce and even vicious battle for survival against weather and disease and poverty some peoples need help. Denied it, they could well become so desperate as to create a world catastrophe.

Now in the ultimate sense, a nation must achieve for itself, by its heart and by its will, the standard of living and the strength needed to progress toward peace with justice and freedom. But where necessary resources and technological skills are lacking, people must be assisted—or all the world will suffer.

In the past, America has been generous. Our generosity has been greeted with gratitude and friendship. On my trip, many millions cried and shouted their testimony to that fact.

No country I visited is short on the greatest of all resources: people of good heart and stout will. And this is especially true of the young. Almost every country is, however, short on the technical knowledge, the skills, the machines, the techniques—and the money—needed to enable their people fully to exploit the natural resources of their lands.

Of course, money alone cannot bring about this progress. Yet America's own best interests, our own hopes for peace, require that we continue our financial investment and aid; and persuade all other free nations to join us—to the limit of their ability—in a long-term program, dependable in its terms and in its duration.

But more importantly, in the spirit of the Christmas season, that there may be peace on earth and good will among men, we must as individuals, as corporations, labor unions, professional societies, as communities, multiply our interest, our concern in these peoples. They are now our warm friends. They will be our stout and strong partners for peace and friendship in freedom if they are given the right sort of help in the right sort of spirit.

The American Government and our allies provide the defensive strength against aggression that permits men of good will to work together for peace. Such strength is an absolute requirement until controlled and safeguarded disarmament allows its reduction, step by step.

Protected by our defensive strength against violent disruption of our peaceful efforts, we are trying to produce a workable, practical program that will make each succeeding Christmas a little closer in spirit and reality to the message of the first Christmas long ago.

This is not a matter of charity for the poverty-stricken nor of easing our own consciences through doles for the distressed. The help we give to our friends is help and strength for the cause of freedom—American freedom—as well as freedom throughout the world.

In giving it, we must be hardheaded but understanding; enlightened in our own interest but sympathetic and generous in the interest of our friends.

Together we should consider all the ways and the forms such help might take. I fervently hope that in this Christmas

Season each of you who is listening will give thought to what you can do for another human, identical with you in his divine origin and destiny, however distant in miles or poor in worldly estate.

With that hope, with that prayer, I wish you all happiness and peace in this season, as I light the nation's Christmas Tree for the Pageant of Peace.

Merry Christmas!

STATE OF THE UNION MESSAGE

TO THE CONGRESS OF THE UNITED STATES

WASHINGTON, D.C., JANUARY 7, 1960

Seven years ago I entered my present office with one long-held resolve overriding all others. I was then, and remain now, determined that the United States shall become an ever more potent resource for the cause of peace. Realizing that peace cannot be for ourselves alone, but for peoples everywhere. This determination is, I know, shared by the entire Congress, indeed, by all Americans.

My purpose today is to discuss some features of America's position, both at home and in her relations to others.

First, I point out that for us, annual self-examination is made a necessity by the fact that we live in a divided world of uneasy equilibrium, with our side committed to its own protection and against aggression by the other.

With both sections of this divided world in possession of unbelievably destructive weapons, mankind approaches a state where mutual annihilation becomes a possibility. No other fact of today's world equals this in importance; it colors everything we say, everything we plan, and everything we do.

There is demanded of us vigilance, determination, and the dedication of whatever portion of our resources to provide adequate security, especially to provide a real deterrent to aggression. These things we are doing. And these facts emphasize the importance of striving incessantly for a just peace.

Only through the strengthening of the spiritual, intellectual, economic, and defensive resources of the free world can we, in confidence, make progress toward this goal.

Second, we note that recent Soviet deportment and pronouncements suggest the possible opening of a somewhat less strained period in the relationships between the Soviet Union and the rest of the world. If these pronouncements be genuine, there is brighter hope of diminishing the intensity of past rivalry and eventually of substituting persuasion for coercion. Whether this is to become an era of lasting promise remains to be tested by actions.

Third, we now stand in the vestibule of a vast new technological age, one that, despite its capacity for human destruction, has an equal capacity to make poverty and human misery obsolete.

Over the past year the Soviet Union has expressed an interest in measures to reduce the common peril of war.

While neither we nor any other free world nation can permit ourselves to be misled by pleasant promises until tested by performance, yet we approach this apparently new opportunity with the utmost seriousness. We must strive to break the calamitous cycle of frustrations and crises which, if unchecked, could spiral into nuclear disaster; the ultimate insanity.

Though the need for dependable agreements to assure against resort to force in settling disputes is apparent to both sides yet as in other issues dividing men and nations, we can-

PRESIDENT EISENHOWER AND PRESIDENT KUBITSCHEK
OF BRAZIL RIDE THROUGH A SHOWER OF TICKER TAPE
IN RIO DE JANEIRO, FEBRUARY, 1960

not expect sudden and revolutionary results. But we must find some place to begin.

One obvious road on which to make a useful start is in the widening of communication between our two peoples. In this field there are, both sides willing, countless opportunities for developing mutual understanding, the true foundation of peace.

Another avenue may be through the reopening, on January 12th, of negotiations looking to a controlled ban on the testing of nuclear weapons. Unfortunately, the closing statement from the Soviet scientists who met with our scientists at Geneva gives the clear impression that their conclusions have been politically guided. Those of the British and American scientific representatives are their own freely formed, individual, and collective opinions. I am hopeful that as new negotiations begin, truth—not political opportunism—will guide the deliberations.

Still another field may be found in the area of disarmament, in which the Soviets have professed a readiness to negotiate seriously. They have not, however, made clear the plans they may have, if any, for mutual inspection and verification—the essential condition for any extensive measure of disarmament.

There is one instance where our initiative for peace has recently been successful. A multi-lateral treaty signed last month provides for the exclusively peaceful use of Antarctica, assured by a system of inspection. It provides for free and co-operative scientific research in that continent, and prohibits nuclear explosions there pending general international agreement on the subject. I shall transmit its text to the Senate for consideration and approval in the near future.

The United States is always ready to participate with the Soviet Union in serious discussion of these or any other subjects that may lead to peace with justice.

Certainly it is not necessary to repeat that the United States has no intention of interfering in the internal affairs of any nation; by the same token, we reject any Soviet attempt to impose its system on us or other peoples by force or subversion.

Now this concern for the freedom of other peoples is the intellectual and spiritual cement which has allied us with more than forty other nations in a common defense effort. Not for a moment do we forget that our own fate is firmly fastened to that of these countries; we will not act in any way which would jeopardize our solemn commitments to them.

We and our friends are, of course, concerned with self-defense. Growing out of this concern is the realization that all people of the Free World have a great stake in the progress, in freedom, of the uncommitted and newly emerging nations. These peoples, desperately hoping to lift themselves to decent levels of living must not, by our neglect, be forced to seek help from, and finally become virtual satellites of, those who proclaim their hostility to freedom.

But they must have technical and investment assistance. This is a problem to be solved not by America alone, but also by every nation cherishing the same ideals and in position to provide help.

In recent years America's partners and friends in Western Europe and Japan have made great economic progress.

The international economy of 1960 is markedly different from that of the early postwar years. No longer is the United States the only major industrial country capable of providing substantial amounts of the resources so urgently needed in the newly developed countries.

To remain secure and prosperous themselves, wealthy nations must extend the kind of co-operation to the less fortunate members that will inspire hope, confidence, and progress. A rich nation can for a time, without noticeable damage to itself, pursue a course of self-indulgence, making its single goal the material ease and comfort of its own citizens—thus repudiating its own spiritual and material stake in a peaceful and prosperous society of nations. But the enmities it will incur, the isolation into which it will descend, and the internal moral and spiritual softness that will be engendered, will, in the long term, bring it to economic and political disaster.

America did not become great through softness and self-indulgence. Her miraculous progress in material achievements flows from other qualities far more worthy and substantial: adherence to principles and methods consonant with our religious philosophy; a satisfaction in hard work; the readiness to sacrifice for worthwhile causes; the courage to meet every challenge; the intellectual honesty and capacity to recognize the true path of her own best interests.

To us and to every nation of the Free World, rich or poor, these qualities are necessary today as never before if we are to march together to greater security, prosperity and peace.

I believe that the industrial countries are ready to participate actively in supplementing the efforts of the developing nations to achieve progress.

The immediate need for this kind of co-operation is underscored by the strain in this nation's international balance of payments. Our surplus from foreign business transactions has in recent years fallen substantially short of the expenditures we make abroad to maintain our military establishments overseas, to finance private investment, and to provide assistance to the less developed nations. In 1959 our deficit in balance of payments approached four billion dollars.

Continuing deficits of anything like this magnitude would, over time, impair our own economic growth and check the forward progress of the Free World.

We must meet this situation by promoting a rising volume of exports and world trade. Further, we must induce all industrialized nations of the Free World to work together to help lift the scourge of poverty from less fortunate. This co-operation in this matter will provide both for the necessary sharing of this burden and in bringing about still further increases in mutually profitable trade.

New Nations, and others struggling with the problems of development, will progress only—regardless of any outside help—if they demonstrate faith in their own destiny and use their own resources to fulfill it. Moreover, progress in a national transformation can be only gradually earned; there is no easy and quick way to follow from the oxcart to the jet plane. But, just as we drew on Europe for assistance in our earlier years, so now do these new and emerging nations that do have this faith and determination deserve help.

Respecting their need, one of the major focal points of our concern is the South-Asian region. Here, in two nations alone, are almost five hundred million people, all working, and working hard, to raise their standards, and in doing so, to make of themselves a strong bulwark against the spread of an ideology that would destroy liberty.

I cannot express to you the depth of my conviction that, in our own and free world interest, we must co-operate with others to help these people achieve their legitimate ambitions, as expressed in their different multi-year plans. Through the World Bank and other instrumentalities, as well as through individual action by every nation in position to help, we must squarely face this titanic challenge.

I shall continue to urge the American people, in the interests of their own security, prosperity and peace, to make sure that their own part of this great project be amply and cheerfully supported. Free world decisions in this matter may spell the difference between world disaster and world progress in freedom.

Other countries, some of which I visited last month, have similar needs.

A common meeting ground is desirable for those nations which are prepared to assist in the development effort. During the past year I have discussed this matter with the leaders of several Western nations.

Because of its wealth of experience, the Organization for European Economic Cooperation could help with the initial studies needed. The goal is to enlist all available economic resources in the industrialized Free World, especially private investment capital.

By extending this help, we hope to make possible the enthusiastic enrollment of these nations under freedom's banner. No more startling contrast to a system of sullen satellites could be imagined.

If we grasp this opportunity to build an age of productive

partnership between the less fortunate nations and those that have already achieved a high state of economic advancement, we will make brighter the outlook for a world order based upon security and freedom. Otherwise, the outlook could be dark indeed. We face, indeed, what may be a turning point in history, and we must act decisively and wisely.

As a nation we can successfully pursue these objectives only from a position of broadly based strength.

No matter how earnest is our quest for guaranteed peace, we must maintain a high degree of military effectiveness at the same time we are engaged in negotiating the issue of arms reduction. Until tangible and mutually enforceable arms reduction measures are worked out we will not weaken the means of defending our institutions.

America possesses an enormous defense power. It is my studied conviction that no nation will ever risk general war against us unless we should become so foolish as to neglect the defense forces we now so powerfully support. It is world-wide knowledge that any power which might be tempted today to attack the United States by surprise, even though we might sustain great losses, would itself promptly suffer a terrible destruction. But I once again assure all peoples and all nations that the United States, except in defense, will never turn loose this destructive power.

During the past year, our long-range striking power, unmatched today in manned bombers, has taken on new strength as the Atlas intercontinental ballistic missile has entered the operational inventory. In fourteen recent test launchings, at ranges of five thousand miles, *Atlas* has been striking on an average within two miles of the target. This is less than the length of a jet runway—well within the circle of destruction. Incidentally, there was an *Atlas* firing last night. From all reports so far received, its performance conformed to the high standards I have just described. Such performance is a great tribute to American scientists and engineers, who in the past five years have had to telescope time and technology to develop these long-range ballistic missiles, where America had none before.

This year, moreover, growing numbers of nuclear powered submarines will enter our active forces, some to be armed with Polaris missiles. These remarkable ships and weapons, ranging the oceans, will be capable of accurate fire on targets virtually anywhere on earth.

To meet situations of less than general nuclear war, we continue to maintain our carrier forces, our many service units abroad, our always ready Army strategic forces and Marine Corps divisions, and the civilian components. The continuing modernization of these forces is a costly but necessary process. It is scheduled to go forward at a rate which will steadily add to our strength.

The deployment of a portion of these forces beyond our shores, on land and sea, is persuasive demonstration of our determination to stand shoulder-to-shoulder with our allies for collective security. Moreover, I have directed that steps be taken to program on a longer range basis our military assistance to these allies. This is necessary for a sounder collective defense system.

Next I refer to our program in space exploration, which is often mistakenly supposed to be an integral part of defense research and development.

We note that, first, America has already made great contributions in the past two years to the world's fund of knowledge of astrophysics and space science. These discoveries are of present interest chiefly to the scientific community; but they are important foundation stones for more extensive exploration of outer space for the ultimate benefit of all mankind.

Second, our military missile program, going forward so successfully, does not suffer from our present lack of very large rocket engines, which are necessary in distant space exploration. I am assured by experts that the thrust of our present missiles is fully adequate for defense requirements.

Third, the United States is pressing forward in the development of large rocket engines to place vehicles of many tons into space for exploration purposes.

Fourth, in the meantime, it is necessary to remember that we have only begun to probe the environment immediately surrounding the earth. Using launch systems presently available, we are developing satellites to scout the world's weather; satellite relay stations to facilitate and extend communications over the globe; for navigation aids to give accurate bearings to ships and aircraft; and for perfecting instruments to collect and transmit the data we seek.

Fifth, we have just completed a year's experience with our new space law. I believe it deficient in certain particulars. Suggested improvements will be submitted to the Congress shortly.

The accomplishment of the many tasks I have alluded to requires the continuous strengthening of the spiritual, intellectual, and economic sinews of American life. The steady purpose of our society is to assure justice, before God, for every individual. We must be ever alert that freedom does not wither through the careless amassing of restrictive controls or the lack of courage to deal boldly with the issues of the day.

A year ago, when I met with you, the nation was emerging from an economic downturn, even though the signs of resurgent prosperity were not then sufficiently convincing to the doubtful. Today our surging strength is apparent to everyone. 1960 promises to be the most prosperous year in our history.

Yet we continue to be afflicted by nagging disorders. Among current problems that require solutions, participated in by citizens as well as government, are:

the need to protect the public interest in situations of prolonged labor-management stalemate;

the persistent refusal to come to grips with a critical problem in one sector of American agriculture;

the continuing threat of inflation, together with the persisting tendency toward fiscal irresponsibility;

in certain instances the denial to some of our citizens of equal protection of the law.

Every American was deeply disturbed by the prolonged dispute in the steel industry and the protracted delay in reaching a settlement.

We are all relieved that a settlement has at last been achieved in that industry. Percentagewise, by this settlement the increase to the steel companies in employment costs is lower than in any prior wage settlement since World War II. It is also gratifying to note that despite the increase in wages and benefits several of the major steel producers have announced that there will be no increase in steel prices at this time. The national interest demands that in the period of industrial peace which has been assured by the new contract, both management and labor make every possible effort to increase efficiency and productivity in the manufacture of steel so that price increases can be avoided.

One of the sharp lessons in this story is that the potential danger to the entire nation of longer and greater strikes must be met. To insure against such possibilities we must of course depend primarily upon the good common sense of the responsible individuals. It is my intention to encourage regular discussions between management and labor outside the bargaining table arena, to consider the interest of the public as well as their own mutual interest in, first, the maintenance of industrial peace, price stability incentives for continuous investment, and economic growth. Both the Executive and the Congress will, I know, be watching developments with the keenest interest.

To me, it seems almost absurd that the United States should recognize the need for, and so earnestly seek, co-operation among the nations unless we can achieve voluntary, dependable, abiding co-operation among the important segments of our own free society. Without such co-operation we cannot prosper.

Failure to face up to basic issues in areas other than those of labor-management can cause serious strains on our society.

Agriculture is one of these areas.

Our basic farm laws were written 27 years ago, in an emergency effort to redress hardship caused by a worldwide depression. They were continued—and their economic distortions intensified—during World War II in order to provide incentives for production of food needed to sustain a war-torn free world.

Today our farm problem is totally different. It is that of effectively adjusting to the changes caused by a scientific revolution. When the original farm laws were written, an hour's farm labor produced only one-fourth as much wheat as the same labor does today. Farm legislation is woefully out-of-date, ineffective, and expensive.

For years we have gone on with an outmoded system which not only has failed to protect farm income, but has produced soaring, threatening surpluses. Our farms have been left producing for war while America has long been at peace.

Once again I urge the Congress to enact legislation that will gear production more closely to markets, make costly surpluses more manageable, provide greater freedom in farm operations, and steadily achieve increased net farm incomes.

Another issue that we must meet squarely is that of living within our means. This requires restraint in expenditure, constant reassessment of priorities, and the maintenance of stable prices.

To do so, we must prevent inflation. Here is an opponent of so many guises that it is sometimes difficult to recognize. But our clear need is to stop continuous and general price rises—a need that all of us can see and feel.

To prevent steadily rising costs and prices calls for stern self-discipline by every citizen. No person, city, state, or organized group can afford to evade the obligation to resist inflation, for every single American pays its crippling tax.

Increases in prices of the goods we sell abroad threaten to

drive us out of markets that once were securely ours. Whether domestic prices, so high as to be noncompetitive, result from demands for too high profit margins or from increased labor costs that outrun growth in productivity, the final result is seriously damaging to the nation.

We must fight inflation as we would fight a fire that imperils our home. Only by so doing can we prevent it from destroying our savings, pensions, and insurance, and from gnawing away the very roots of a free, healthy economy and the nation's security.

One major method by which the Federal government can counter rising prices is to insure that its own expenditures are below its revenues. The debt with which we are now confronted is about two hundred and ninety billion dollars. With interest charges alone now costing taxpayers about nine and one-half billions each year, it is clear that this debt growth must stop. You will be glad to know that despite the unsettling influences of the recent steel strike, we estimate that our accounts will show, on June 30, this year, a favorable balance of approximately two hundred million dollars.

I shall, beyond this, I shall present to the Congress for 1961 a balanced budget. It provides that in the area of defense, expenditures continue at record peacetime levels. With a single exception, expenditures in every major category of Health, Education and Welfare will be equal or greater than those of last year. In Space expenditures the amounts are practically doubled. But the over-all guiding goal of this budget is national need—not response to specific group, local or political insistence.

Expenditure increases, other than those I have indicated,

are largely accounted for by the increased cost of legislation previously enacted.

I repeat, this budget will be a balanced one. Expenditures will be seventy-nine billion, eight hundred million dollars. The amount of income over outgo, described in the budget as a surplus to be applied against our national debt, is four billion, two hundred million dollars. Personally, I do not feel that any amount can be properly called a "surplus" as long as the nation is in debt. I prefer to think of such an item as "reduction on our children's inherited mortgage." And once we have established such payments as normal practice, we can profitably make improvements in our tax structure and thereby truly reduce the heavy burdens of taxation. In any event, this one reduction will save taxpayers each year approximately two hundred million dollars in interest costs.

This favorable balance will ease pressure in our credit and capital markets. It will enhance the confidence of people all over the world in the strength of our economy and our currency.

In the management of the huge public debt the Treasury is unfortunately not free of artificial barriers. Its ability to deal with the difficult problems in this field has been weakened greatly by the unwillingness of the Congress to remove archaic restrictions. The need for a freer hand in debt management is even more urgent today because the costs of the undesirable financing measures which the Treasury has been forced into are steadily mounting. Removal of this roadblock has high priority in my legislative recommendations.

Still another issue relates to civil rights.

In all our hopes and plans for a better world we all recognize that provincial and racial prejudices must be combatted. In the long perspective of history, the right of the vote has been one of the strongest pillars of any free society. Our first duty is to protect this right against all encroachment. In spite of constitutional guarantees, and notwithstanding much progress of recent years, bias still deprives some persons in this country of equal protection of the laws.

Early in your last session, I recommended legislation which would help eliminate several practices discriminating against the basic rights of Americans. The Civil Rights Commission has developed additional constructive recommendations. I hope that these will be among the matters to be seriously considered in the current session. I trust that Congress will thus signal to the world that our Government is striving for equality under law for all our people.

Each year and in many ways our nation continues to undergo profound change and growth.

In the past eighteen months, we have hailed the entry of two more States of the Union, Alaska and Hawaii. We proudly salute these two western stars.

Our vigorous expansion, which we all welcome as a sign of health and vitality, is many-sided. We are, for example, witnessing explosive growth in metropolitan areas.

The roster of urban problems with which they must cope is staggering. They involve water supply, cleaning the air, adjusting local tax systems, providing for essential educational, cultural, and social services, and destroying those conditions which breed delinquency and crime.

In meeting these, we must, if we value our historic freedoms, keep within the traditional framework of our Federal system with powers divided between the national and state governments.

I do not doubt that our urban and other perplexing problems can be solved in the traditional American method. In doing so we must realize that nothing is really solved but ruinous tendencies are set in motion by yielding to the deceptive bait of the "easy" Federal tax dollar.

Our educational system provides a ready example.

We cannot be complacent about educating our youth. All recognize the vital necessity for modern school plants and well-qualified and adequately compensated teachers, but the route to better trained minds is not through the swift administration of a Federal hypodermic or even sustained financial transfusion. The educational process, essentially a local and personal responsibility, cannot be made to leap ahead by crash, centralized governmental action.

The Administration has proposed a carefully reasoned plan for helping eliminate current deficiencies. It is designed to stimulate such things as classroom construction, not by substitution of Federal dollars for state and local funds, but by incentives to extend and encourage state and local efforts. This approach rejects the notion of Federal domination or control. And it is workable, and should appeal to every American interested in advancement of our educational system in the traditional American way. I urge the Congress to take action upon this plan.

There is one other subject concerning which I renew a recommendation I made in my *State of the Union Message* last January. I then advised the Congress of my purpose to intensify our efforts to replace force with a rule of law among nations. That purpose is widely and deeply shared by many other peoples and nations of the world.

In the same Message, I stated that our efforts would include a re-examination of our own relation to the International Court of Justice. The Court was established to decide international legal disputes between nations. In 1946 we accepted the Court's jurisdiction, but subject to a reservation of the right to determine unilaterally whether a matter lies essentially within domestic jurisdiction. There is pending before the Senate, a Resolution which would repeal our present self-judging reservation. I support that Resolution and urge its prompt passage. If this is done, I intend to urge similar acceptance of the Court's jurisdiction by every member of the United Nations.

Here perhaps it is not amiss for me to say a personal word to the Members of the Congress, in this my final year of office.

I am not unique as a President who has worked with a Congress controlled by the opposition party—except that no other President ever did it quite so long! Yet in both personal and official relationships we have weathered all the storms of the past five years. And for this I am deeply grateful.

My deep concern in the next twelve months, before my successor takes office, is with our joint Congressional-Executive duty to our own and to other nations. Acting upon the beliefs I have expressed here today, I shall devote my full energies to the tasks at hand. Presumably this will involve travel for promoting greater world understanding, negotiations to reduce international discord, or constant discussions and communications with the Congress and the American people to settle issues both domestic and foreign.

In pursuit of these objectives, I look forward to, and rededicate myself to, a close and constructive association with the Congress.

We seek a common goal: brighter opportunity for our own citizens and a world peace with justice for all.

Before us and our friends is the challenge of an ideology which, for more than four decades, has trumpeted abroad its purpose of gaining ultimate victory over all forms of government at variance with its own.

We realize that however much we repudiate the tenets of imperialistic Communism, it represents a gigantic enterprise. Its leaders compel its subjects to subordinate their freedom of action and spirit and personal desires in favor of some hoped for advantage in the future.

And the Communists can present an array of material accomplishments over the past fifteen years that lends a false persuasiveness to many of their glittering promises to the uncommitted peoples.

The competition they provide is formidable. We so recognize it.

But in our scale of values we place freedom first. Our whole national development has been geared to that basic concept and is responsible for the position of free world leadership to which we have succeeded.

Freedom is the highest prize that any nation can possess; it is one that Communism can never offer. And America's record of material accomplishment in freedom is written not only in the unparalleled prosperity of our own nation, it is found also in the many billions we have devoted to the reconstruction of Free World economies wrecked by World War II and in the effective help provided by many more billions we have given in saving the independence of numerous others threatened by outside domination. Assuredly we have the capacity for handling the problems in the new era of the world's history we are now entering.

But we must use that capacity intelligently, tirelessly, and regardless of personal sacrifice.

The fissure that divides our political planet is deep and wide.

We live, moreover, in a storm of semantic disorder in which old labels no longer faithfully describe. Police states are called "people's democracies." Armed conquest of free people is called "liberation." Such slippery slogans make difficult the problem of communicating true faiths, facts and beliefs. So doing, we must use language to enlighten the mind, not as the instrument of the studied innuendo and distorter of truth. And we must live by what we say.

As a nation we take pride that our own constitutional system, and the ideals which sustain it, have been long viewed elsewhere as a fountainhead of freedom. By our every word and action we must strive to make ourselves worthy of this trust, ever mindful that an accumulation of seemingly minor encroachments upon freedom gradually could break down the entire fabric of a free society.

So persuaded, we shall get on with the task before us.

So dedicated, and with faith in the Almighty, humanity shall one day achieve the unity in freedom to which all men have aspired from the dawn of time.

THE AMERICAN REPUBLICS

ADDRESS PRIOR TO DEPARTURE FOR SOUTH AMERICA

WASHINGTON, D.C., FEBRUARY 21, 1960

Early tomorrow I start a journey to several of our Latin American neighbors, with three major purposes in mind. These are: to learn more about our friends to the south; to assure them again that the United States seeks to co-operate with them in achieving a fuller life for everyone in this hemisphere; and to make clear our desire to work closely with them in the building of a universal peace with justice.

Our interest in our sister Republics is of long standing, and of deep affection. This, in itself, is reason sufficient for the journey. But in these days of world tension, of awakening ambitions, and of problems caused by the growing interdependence of nations, it is vital for national partners to develop better understandings and to improve common programs.

The bonds among our American Republics are not merely geographic; rather they are shared principles and convictions. Together we believe in God, in the dignity and rights of man, in peace with justice, and in the right of every people to determine its own destiny. In such beliefs our friendship is rooted.

Yet even among close comrades, friendships too often seem to be taken for granted. We must not give our neighbors of Latin America cause to believe this about us.

So I shall affirm to our sister Republics that we are steadfast in our purpose to work with them hand in hand in promoting the security and well-being of all peoples of this hemisphere.

To do so, calls for a sustained effort that is, unfortunately, sometimes impeded by misunderstandings.

One such misunderstanding, at times voiced in Latin America, is that we have been so preoccupied with the menace of Communist imperialism and resulting problems of defense, that we have tended to forget our southern neighbors. Some have implied that our attention has been so much directed to security for ourselves and to problems across the oceans to the west and east, that we neglect co-operation and progress within this hemisphere.

It is true that we have given first priority to world-wide measures for security against the possibility of military aggression. We have made many sacrifices to assure that this security is and will be maintained.

But I hope to make clear, on my journey, that our military programs at home and abroad have been designed for one purpose only—the maintenance of peace, as important to Latin America as to us.

That there is need for these programs, postwar history clearly proves.

For the first five years following World War II, we in the United States, hopeful of a global and durable peace, pursued a policy of virtual disarmament. But, the blockade of Berlin, the military weakness of our European friends living face to face with the Communist menace, and finally the Korean War—together with arrogant threats against other peaceful nations—belatedly made it clear to us that only under an umbrella of military strength could free nations hope to make progress toward an enduring and just peace. World uneasiness rose to the point of alarm.

Since then our nation has developed great arsenals of powerful weapons to sustain the peace. We have created a great deterrent strength, so powerful as to command and to justify the respect of knowledgeable and unbiased observers here at home and abroad.

Our many hundreds of Air Force bombers deployed the world over, each capable of unleashing a frightful destruction, constitute a force far superior to any other, in numbers, in quality, and in strategic location of bases. We have, in addition, a powerful nuclear force in our aircraft carriers and in our host of widely deployed tactical aircraft. Adding constantly to these forces are advanced types of missiles steadily augmenting the armaments of all ground and other military units.

As for longer range ballistic missiles, from a standing start only five years ago, we have literally leaped forward in accomplishments no less than remarkable. Our *Atlas* missile, already amazingly accurate, became operational last year. Missiles of intermediate range are in forward bases. The first *Polaris* missile submarine, an almost invulnerable weapon, will soon be at sea. New generations of long range missiles are under urgent development.

Collectively, this is a force not unduly dependent upon any one weapon or any one service, not subject to elimination by sudden attack, buttressed by an industrial system unmatched on this earth, and unhesitatingly supported by a vigorous people determined to remain free. Strategically, that force is far better situated than any other that could be brought to bear against us.

As we have strengthened these defenses, we have helped to bolster our own and free world security by assisting in arming forty-two other nations—our associates in the defense of the free world. Our part in this indispensable effort is our Mutual Security Program. It makes possible a forward strategy of defense for the greater security of all, including our neighbors to the south.

I am certain that our Latin American neighbors, as well as you here at home, understand the significance of all these facts.

We have forged a trustworthy shield of peace; an indestructible force of incalculable power, ample for today and constantly developing to meet the needs of tomorrow. Today, in the presence of continuous threat, all of us can stand resolute and unafraid—confident in America's might as an anchor of free world security.

But we all recognize that peace and freedom cannot be forever sustained by weapons alone. There must be a free world spirit and morale based upon the conviction that, for free men, life comprehends more than mere survival and bare security. Peoples everywhere must have opportunity to better themselves spiritually, intellectually, economically.

We earnestly seek to help our neighbors in this hemisphere achieve the progress they rightly desire.

We have sought to strengthen the Organization of American States and other co-operative groups which promote hemispheric progress and solidarity.

We have invested heavily in Latin American enterprise.

New credits, both public and private, are being made available in greater volume than ever before. Last year, these approximated one billion dollars. Our outstanding loans and investments in Latin America now exceed eleven billion dollars.

With our sister Republics, we have just established the InterAmerican Development Bank. With them we hope that this new billion dollar institution will do much to accelerate economic growth.

Additionally, we have expanded technical co-operation programs throughout the Americas.

To improve our own knowledge of our neighbors' needs, we recently established a distinguished panel of private citizens under the chairmanship of the Secretary of State. This National Advisory Committee will, by continuous study of inter-American affairs, help us at home better to co-operate with our Latin American friends. Members of this Committee will accompany me on my journey tomorrow.

This will be a busy trip, for our neighbors' problems are many and vexing: the lack of development capital; wide fluctuations in the prices of their export commodities; the need for common regional markets to foster efficiency and to attract new credits; the need to improve health, education, housing, and transportation.

All these are certain to be subjects of discussion in each of the countries I visit. And wherever I go, I shall state again and again the basic principles and attitudes that govern our country's relationships in this hemisphere.

For example:

Our good partner policy is a permanent guide, encompassing nonintervention, mutual respect, and juridical equality of States.

We wish, for every American nation, a rapid economic progress, with its blessings reaching all the people.

We are always eager to co-operate in fostering sound development within the limits of practical capabilities; further, we shall continue to urge every nation to join in help to the less fortunate.

We stand firmly by our pledge to help maintain the security of the Americas under the Rio Treaty of 1947.

We declare our faith in the rule of law, our determination to abide by treaty commitments, and our insistence that other nations do likewise.

We will do all we can to foster the triumph of human liberty throughout the hemisphere.

We condemn all efforts to undermine the democratic institutions of the Americas through coercion or subversion, and we abhor the use of the lie and distortion in relations among nations.

Very recently, in a faraway country that has never known freedom—one which today holds millions of humans in subjugation—impassioned language has been used to assert that the United States has held Latin America in a colonial relationship to ourselves.

That is a blatant falsehood.

In all history no nation has had a more honorable record in its dealings with other countries than has the United States.

The Philippines are independent today—by their own choice.

Alaska and Hawaii are now proud partners in our federated, democratic enterprise—by their own choice.

Puerto Rico is a Commonwealth within the United States system—by its own choice.

After the two world wars and the Korean War, the

United States did not annex a single additional acre, and it has sought no advantage of any kind at the expense of another.

And in all of Latin America, I repeat, we adhere honorably and persistently to the policy of nonintervention.

It is nonsense to charge that we hold—or that we desire to hold—any nation in colonial status.

These are but a few of the matters that friends in this hemisphere need to talk about. I look forward with the keenest pleasure to exchanging views with the Presidents of Brazil, Argentina, Chile, and Uruguay, and with their colleagues.

It is my profound hope that, upon my return, I shall be able to repeat to you that the historic friendship and trust among the nations of this hemisphere have been strengthened, and that our common cause—justice and peace in freedom—has been reaffirmed and given new life.

VISION OF TRUE FREEDOM

I am honored by this opportunity to address the Congress of the Argentine Republic. To you, and through you to all your people, I bring friendly greetings from my government and my fellow citizens. I convey to you our unbounded admiration for the courageous efforts you are making under the inspired leadership of President Frondizi to strengthen respect for human dignity and human rights, and to build institutions which will eternally guarantee the free exercise of those rights.

Though the peoples of the United States do not know your history, philosophy, and aspirations as well as they should—and this is a serious shortcoming which, despite distance and dissimilar language, simply must be overcome. Nonetheless they are mindful of the extraordinary efforts you are making to restore your national economy. We hope and expect that the solid economic foundations you have been building will soon result in improved living standards.

I am happy that Argentina has created conditions which have made it possible for some of our credit agencies to extend to it a significant program of dollar credits. During the last few years, public and private lending agencies of the

United States, and international financial institutions to which we contribute substantially, have joined in lending to Argentina approximately a billion dollars. This is the most intensive program of financial co-operation to have been carried out in the history of the Hemisphere.

In a nation that is truly determined to develop, capital is one essential instrument of production. If there is a shortage of capital, production and living standards suffer simultaneously. New capital, if accompanied by other instruments of production including technical proficiency—in this case provided by Argentina—is quickly translated into more production, more and better paid jobs, and higher living standards. Everybody gains in the process.

We of the United States are proud that we have been able to assist in your march toward a better life.

In words so candid and clear that no one in all the Americas can possibly misunderstand me, I wish to emphasize again our deep desire:

First, to see everyone of the American nations make steady economic progress, with the blessing of this advance reaching all its people.

Second, to co-operate in every sound way we can within the limits of our ability, in helping the American nations attain their just aspirations, and to persuade them and others to join in a world-wide effort to help the less developed nations progress in freedom.

Third, while adhering strictly to a policy of nonintervention and mutual respect, to applaud the triumph of free self-government everywhere in the world. We do not urge emulation of the United States, but we know that human beings, sacred in the sight of God and more majestic than any institution they may create, will in the long sweep of history never be content with any form of slavery or coercion.

Fourth, to bring ever closer the realization of a world in which peace with freedom is guaranteed, and in which the mighty productive power of man can work constructively for the betterment of all humankind.

As perhaps you know, I have recently traveled to Europe, the Middle East, and India. I am now at the half-way point in this all-too-brief trip through South America. In June I shall go to the Soviet Union and Japan. When those journeys have been completed, I shall have visited many countries, large and small, industrial and agricultural communities, highly developed nations and some newly emerging. In all these travels I have had one paramount interest: to assure everybody of my nation's peaceful intent and to do what I can to promote the co-operation of all in the cause of peace with freedom.

I have emphasized that we seek peace, but only in freedom. If peoples were willing to give up their liberty and their personal dignity, they could readily have peace—a peace in which a single great power controlled all other nations.

Ghengis Khan, Tamerlane, Alexander the Great, Napoleon, Hitler, and others sought to establish that kind of peace. But always peoples and nations have rebelled against their false, self-serving doctrines. We do not want an imposed peace. We want, rather, a co-operative peace in which the peoples of every nation have the right of free choice, the right to establish their own institutions, to live by their own cardinal concepts and to be free of external pressure or threat.

These are deep-seated desires held passionately in common by the peoples of the United States and Argentina. We share a consuming wish for a just peace, in freedom, and together we hope to have machines capable of destruction turned exclusively to constructive purposes.

These shared aspirations spring from a common heritage.

Both our countries won their independence from European powers. The drafters of our Declaration of Independence proclaimed that all men are created equal, endowed by their Creator with certain equal, inalienable rights, among them life, liberty, and the pursuit of happiness. In Argentina, Esteban Echeverria said: "Equality and liberty are . . . the two poles of . . . democracy." In the United States, Abraham Lincoln described democratic government as "of the people, by the people and for the people."

In Argentina, Juan B. Alberdi declared: "Public freedom is no more than the sum . . . of the freedoms of all." The Constitution of the United States carefully separated the legislative, executive, and judicial branches of our Government. In Argentina, the great liberator, Jose de San Martin, stated: "Displaying the most excellent principles matters not at all when he who makes the law, he who carries it out, is also he who judges it."

Your founding fathers and ours acted upon the same great hopes and expressed almost identically the same wisdom. This is, of course, not surprising: The vision of true freedom cannot be dimmed by a barrier of language or distance.

It was once possible to think of democratic freedom as a matter of purely national concern. But now, in a world of exacting interdependence, freedom must be fostered, developed, and maintained co-operatively among many nations. Hence across national boundaries, among peoples and governments, a constant increase in mutual understanding must prevail.

Based on that understanding, political, cultural, and economic co-operation will succeed, with benefits for all.

Unhappily, until the last threat of force has been suppressed, there must also be military co-operation, for no single nation, no matter how mighty, can alone protect the freedom of all. Together, however, the nations which cherish independence can command a power so great that no potential aggressor could violate the peace without destruction.

Can the ugly external threat which faces us impose such physical strains upon us as to impair or destroy our heritage? With confidence we jointly say, "No." I have heard some say that the more a country develops its technology and science, the more "materialistic" it becomes, and the less it possesses or cherishes the cultural aspects of life. But of course science, technology, and richness of culture must, and do, march forward hand in hand.

Surely scientific advances that make possible the conquering of human disease, that remove drudgery from the household, that yield shorter working hours with leisure for music and play—surely these are not inimical to the fulfillment of man's spiritual aspirations.

No single technological development in all history did more to advance the cultures of the world than the invention of the printing press. Modern technological miracles have speeded communications to the point that an event in a remote part of Africa is known minutes later in Buenos

Aires. They have enabled us to move from one part of the world to any other in a matter of hours.

With these so-called "materialistic" advances, we have the means of obtaining accurate information and more knowledge faster. These accomplishments are helpful in developing that genuine human understanding on which all other co-operative actions among peace-longing nations can be based.

I have watched, with much satisfaction, the increasing amount of news published in each of our countries about the other; and the increasing number of books translated from each of our languages into the other's. I have observed, too, the growing numbers of our teachers, students, business men, labor leaders, and others who are exchanging visits.

My country was recently honored by the visit of a number of distinguished members of this Congress, who traveled extensively in the United States and conferred with their fellow legislators and other American citizens. Also, legislators from the United States have visited Argentina on numerous occasions. I can think of nothing more useful to our relations than such exchanges.

But it is not possible for everyone to travel great distances. So our schools and universities, the press, books, philosophic societies, study groups and Government—all these must work ceaselessly to promote better understanding between us as well as among all the Americas.

And there must be interchanges to the maximum degree possible of ideas, of persons, of techniques.

I hold the unshakeable conviction that the greatest single

impediment to abiding, mutually helpful co-operation among nations desiring peace with freedom is not opposing policies or different aspirations or insoluble conflicts—serious as these sometimes are. No, the most persistent single impediment to healthy, effective co-operation is the lack of deep and abiding understanding, and the mistrust that flows from misunderstanding. In the effort to increase mutual understanding among all nations, here is the basic problem. It is one that every citizen, in your country and mine, can help solve. Overcoming it will build the surest foundation for the kind of co-operative progress we all seek.

Again, I convey to you the admiration of the people of the United States for the courage and determination with which Argentina is facing its problems. We wish you every success. I am also happy to assure you of the continued readiness of my Government to co-operate with you to the extent that such co-operation is feasible, is welcomed and may contribute to the well-being of your great country.

FOR A FIRMER PARTNERSHIP

My first words upon my return from the four American republics I have just visited must be a heartfelt expression of gratitude for the friendly receptions my associates and I experienced, wherever we went.

Millions endured for long hours along the streets the hot summer sun, and occasionally rain, to let us know of the enthusiastic good will they have for the government and people of the United States. In the nations of Latin America—indeed as I have found in all of the eighteen countries I have visited in my trips of recent months—there is a vast reservoir of respect, admiration, and affection for the United States of America. The expressions of this attitude by Latin American peoples and their leaders were so enthusiastic and so often repeated as to admit no possibility of mistake. Two or three insignificant exceptions to this may have made a headline, but they were only minor incidents, lost in the massed welcome.

This was a good will trip, but it was also much more. Members of my party and I held serious conversations and exchanged information on bilateral, hemispheric, and global problems with the four Heads of States, with Cabinet members, with leaders of labor, education, finance, and business.

Two impressions are highlighted in my mind.

First, Brazil, Argentina, Chile, and Uruguay treasure as

much as we do freedom, human dignity, equality, and peace with justice. In freedom, they are determined to progress; to improve and diversify their economies; to provide better housing and education; to work ceaselessly for rising levels of human well being.

Second, while certain problems are continental in scope, nonetheless each of the countries I visited, indeed, each of the twenty republics of Latin America, is highly individual. Each has its own unique problems and ideas regarding future development.

Hence, our co-operation with each republic must be tailored to its particular situation.

I was gratified to learn that, as the indispensable basis for their self-improvement, comprehensive surveys of resources, capacities, objectives, and costs have progressed rapidly in recent years. But each nation feels it must do more in this regard, and seeks help for this purpose. The United Nations has funds for such predevelopment studies. The new Inter-American Bank also should be able to lend technical help. The studies of each country called for under "Operation Pan America" will likewise contribute to this end.

Once sound planning has made significant progress, a nation can formulate specific projects for action, with priorities established, and with confidence that each development will open still further opportunity to speed the spiral of growth.

The execution of any development program will of course depend primarily upon the dedicated efforts of the peoples themselves.

I was impressed, for example, by what I saw in Chile. I visited a low-cost housing project. The government had provided land and utilities. The home owners were helping one another build the new houses. They will pay for them monthly, over a period of years. Personal accomplishments brought pride to their eyes; self-reliance to their bearing. Their new homes are modest in size and character; but I cannot possibly describe the intense satisfaction they take in the knowledge that they themselves have brought about this great forward step in their living conditions.

In Argentina and Uruguay I witnessed encouraging sights —men building schools, homes, and roads—and, in Brazil, erecting a wholly new capital city.

The people of Latin America know that poverty, ignorance, and ill-health are not inevitable. They are determined to have their resources and labors yield a better life for themselves and for their children.

I assured them that most earnestly, we of the United States want them to succeed. We realize that to speed improvement, they need foreign capital. They want sound loans, public and private. Their repayment record on loans previously made is noteworthy.

International and United States lending agencies have recently had their funds greatly increased. The new Inter-American Development Bank will soon be functioning. I believe that each nation which has produced a well-conceived development program will find that these lending institutions will respond to their needs. Should this not be so in a particular situation, we of the United States would want to know the circumstances and do what we could to help rectify the difficulty.

In our discussions, I stressed that all nations—large or small, powerful or weak—should assume some responsibility for the advancement of humankind, in freedom. Though we of the United States will, within the framework of our world situation and economic capacity, assist all we can, we look for the time when all the free nations will feel a common responsibility for our common destiny. Co-operation among free nations is the key to common progress. Aid from one to another, if on a one way street basis only, and indefinitely continued, is not of itself truly productive.

The peoples of Latin America appreciate that our assistance in recent years has reached new heights, and that this has required sacrifice on our part.

I must repeat, however, what I said several times during my trip: Serious misunderstandings of the United States do exist in Latin America. And, indeed, we are not as well informed of them as we should be.

Many persons do not realize the United States is just as committed as are the other republics to the principles of the Rio Treaty of 1947. This Treaty declares that an attack on one American republic will in effect be an attack on all. We stand firmly by this commitment. This mutual security system, proved by time, should now enable some of the American republics to reduce expenditures for armaments, and thus make funds available for constructive purposes.

One editorial alleged that the United States did not accept the principle of nonintervention until 1959. In fact, our country has consistently abided by this hemispheric concept for more than a quarter of a century.

Another persistent misunderstanding which I sought to correct wherever I traveled is that we sometimes support dictators. Of course we abhor all tyrannical forms of government, whether of the left or of the right. This I made clear.

In Brazil, I explained another important item of our policy: We believe in the rights of people to choose their own form of government, to build their own institutions, to abide by their own philosophy. But if a tyrannical form of government were imposed upon any of the Americas from outside or with outside support—by force, threat, or subversion— we would certainly deem this to be a violation of the principle of nonintervention and would expect the Organization of American States, acting under pertinent solemn commitments, to take appropriate collective action.

On occasion I heard it said that economic advance in some American republics only makes the rich richer, and the poor poorer, and that the United States should take the initiative in correcting this evil. This is a view fomented by Communists, but often repeated by well-meaning people.

If there should be any truth in this charge whatsoever, it is not the fault of the United States. So far as our purpose is involved, projects financed by our institutions are expected to yield widespread benefits to all, and at the same time to conform to our policy of nonintervention. I know that the Latin American leaders I met also seek this same result.

Moreover, when internal social reform is required, it is purely an internal matter.

One of the most far-reaching problems of continental scope is this: in their exports, the Latin American republics are largely single commodity countries. The world market prices of what they sell fluctuate widely, whereas the prices of things they buy keep going up.

We have tried to be helpful in the co-operative study of this vexing situation. Many facts about supply, demand, production are widely comprehended for the first time. Thus, for example, with the facts about coffee understood, producing nations are co-operating in orderly marketing for this commodity with beneficial results.

The real solution is in agricultural and industrial diversification. Here, we are encouraged by the progress being made toward the creation of common markets. Large areas, relatively free of trade restrictions, will make for greater efficiency in production and distribution, and will attract new capital to speed development.

Despite such problems as these, our relationships with our sister republics have, with notable but very few exceptions, reached an all-time high. Leaders and populations alike attested to this truth. But an even firmer partnership must be our goal.

The republics of this hemisphere have a special relationship to one another. The United States is important to all of Latin America, as its largest buyer, as the main source of foreign investment capital, and as a bastion of freedom. Our southern neighbors are important to us, economically, politically, culturally, militarily. Indeed, no other area of the world is of more vital significance to our own future.

This interdependence must be comprehended by us, and by them. Each should know the policies, attitudes, aspirations, and capacities of the other. For, as I have said time and again, all fruitful, abiding co-operation must be based upon genuine mutual understanding of vital facts.

Exchanges of students, teachers, labor leaders, and others are helpful. Newspapers, magazines, all means of communication should accept the responsibility not merely of transmitting spectacular news, but of helping build the knowledge on which co-operative action may flourish.

In one respect our neighbors put us to shame. English is

rapidly spreading as the second language in Latin America. Business executives, labor leaders, taxi drivers—most speak English well, learned in school or in binational institutes. The study of Spanish is increasing in our schools, but I wish that literally millions of Americans would learn to speak Spanish or Portuguese fluently, and to read the literature, histories, and periodicals of our sister republics.

H. G. Wells once said that civilization is a race between education and catastrophe. His thought is applicable to hemispheric relations. With common dedication to the highest ideals of mankind, including shared aspirations for a world at peace, freedom, and progress, there is no insurmountable impediment to fruitful co-operation, save only insufficiency in mutual understanding. This is something that you and I, every single citizen, simply by informing himself can do something about.

I hope each of us will do so.

Again, I express my gratitude to President Kubitschek, President Frondizi, President Alessandri, and President Nardone and all their peoples for providing me with a most instructive and rewarding experience.

SOVIET-AMERICAN RELATIONS

When in 1945 I was in Russia, my stay necessarily had to be short. Nevertheless, I then insisted that I could not return to my post of duty in Berlin until I had paid homage to the valiant defenders of Leningrad against Nazi outrage. After fifteen years' absence, I return here more firmly convinced than ever that this city is a world landmark, an enduring monument to the noblest of human traits—superb heroism and cultural progress.

Through many months, the men and women and children of Leningrad withstood siege guns and bombers and swarming armies; hunger and disease and violent death. The whole world watched them through winter months and summer months and winter months again. They wrote for mankind to read, even centuries from now, an epic of courage and sacrifice and unfaltering faith.

In the passage of years, the stones of your city may wear away; the physical image of Leningrad may alter. But wherever men honor the brave and the resolute, never will the memory of the evil siege and the glorious triumph be forgotten.

So today, foremost in my thoughts, even as fifteen years ago this summer, is a salute from the heart to the greatness of Leningrad—to the epic its people wrote in the annals of heroism.

Not by an iota have the years diminished my respect and admiration for the heroes of Leningrad. Quite the contrary. But I must assert as strongly as I can that many of the hopes I then nourished have faded; many of the fears I then tried to brush away have been realized.

Only a few months before my visit here in that year of Russia's and America's mutual triumph, I wrote to the Allied troops who served with me this sentence in an Order of the Day: "Let us have no part in the profitless quarrels in which other men will inevitably engage as to what country, what service, won the European war."

Worse than profitless quarrels have come to pass. Suspicion and rancor and fear, voiced often in the harshest words of threat, too often mark the relations of peoples once tightly joined in a common cause and by a common victory. All of us are at fault that there have been such tragic crimes against friendship.

But our fault will be the most tragic of all crimes if we shrug our shoulders and say, "This sort of thing has always happened"; if we fail, you and I, all of us, to act positively and vigorously that suspicion and rancor and fear be banished.

When I was a boy, we put blinders on horses so they would not shy in fright of a scarecrow, a shadow, a rabbit. But today we human beings deliberately put blinders on ourselves, not to avoid the sight of frightful things, but to ignore a central fact of human existence.

I mean that mankind too often blinds itself to the common lot, to the common purposes, to the common aspirations of humanity everywhere. I mean that all of us too much live in ignorance of our neighbors; or, when we take off our blinders, view them through the contortionist spectacles of propaganda.

And we will continue that way—forever fearful, forever suspicious—until we convince ourselves that the only way to peace is through the mutually open society. Then, at long last, seeing our human neighbors as they really are, we shall come to realize that we need no more fear them than the horse the rabbit.

So I come to this home of heroes with a feeling of inescapable duty upon me to understand better your achievements, your concerns, your beliefs, and your hopes—the great and good you share with all your country.

To reach such understanding is a compelling duty on all Americans; on myself and on my 181 million fellow citizens. To ignore it is as senseless as to read only the odd-numbered pages in a book.

And what applies to Americans should apply to Russians, too. What is sauce for the goose is sauce for the gander.

Your warm welcome assures me that we can find ways better to understand each other. I hope that you will come to my country in tens of thousands, as Americans have come here, to see and examine our way of life in America.

If you travel over America in our jets you will see *all* America. Our country is not as large as yours. It is crossed and criss-crossed by commercial air lanes. At forty thousand feet on a clear day, nothing can be hidden from a citizen or a visitor who wants to look; miles of countryside lie exposed on either side of the plane. And we don't prohibit cameras or binoculars. Were we to do that, my desk would be buried under complaints from outraged camera fans; the manufacturers and sellers of film and optical wares would give me no rest.

But, most important of all, we would hope you could see the vigor with which our Republic grows and changes. So seeing you would understand, I think, that our way of life is not destined to wither and to be buried in the limbo of history's failures. You would understand, I think, that there is no single inevitable system that will envelop the earth.

And my first compelling duty is matched by another: to assure, to persuade, to convince you that above all else the American people want in this world and in their lives peace with all nations; a peace strong in mutual understanding; a peace warm with friendship; a peace enjoyed in freedom— freedom from war and its threat; freedom from propaganda and its hate; freedom from man-made curtains and walls of every sort that make nations ignorant, suspicious, fearful of each other.

My purpose is not one of debate; but as we welcomed Premier Khrushchev in our nation to describe to us the ideals, procedures, and forms of the Soviet system, I shall, without criticism of that system, try to explain the aspirations, principles, and methods on which we operate.

To no more fitting place can I come for the discharge of this duty. Peter, who founded this city, thought of it as a "Window on the West."

Today, I ask you and all Russia to look through your window across eight thousand miles of land and water to my homeland. As you look, I ask that you forget for the moment this or that incident whose nearness in time magnifies and distorts its significance. I ask you instead to remember more than seventeen long decades of friendly, co-operative, profitable relations between our two people.

Remember an American naval hero who became a Russian admiral.

Remember a Russian fleet entering our largest port to hearten and encourage the American Republic in a dark hour when its survival was at stake.

Remember, as we Americans proudly remember, the Russian discovery and exploration and settlement of the forty-ninth State in our Union, Alaska; and how in the most peaceful and friendly of international transactions Russia added half a million square miles to American territory.

Remember the tens upon tens of thousands of Russians who, before your Revolution, found in our ports gateways to freedom from the oppression of tyrants—and a warm, friendly welcome from America.

Remember the hundreds of war-time ships, full-laden with arms and food, sailing to Russia from many American ports. Remember they sailed so that you, who had spent your blood and your treasure in a righteous war, might gain new strength to reach Torgau on the Elbe where Russians and Americans embraced—comrades in arms; partners in victory.

As you look and as you recall those years, I ask that you try better to understand that we Americans seek of you only your co-operation in establishing a peace in which you and we, and every other people, can develop our destinies in freedom.

As I attempt the discharge of these two duties: to convince you of America's decent purposes; to learn and better to understand your way, I have in my mind the words of a distinguished Russian who counselled the American people in an address delivered in Chicago more than sixty years ago. He was Prince Serge Wolkonsky (Sergiei Mikhailovich Volkonskii). Permit me to read a paragraph from his talk:

When you want to learn what a nation is, what a nation is capable of, when you want to know her ideas, her aspirations, her character, when you want to know a nation's soul,—do not study her from the reports of the daily papers or the cheap pamphlets which are written for one occasion and the fame of which lasts but a month or two. Learn a nation from the precious contributions she has given to the eternal treasures of humanity; learn her from what she did for universal science, universal art; learn to know the nation from her beacons, from those men she is proud of, and first of all—let politics alone.

So spoke Serge Wolkonsky. We Americans strive to heed his counsel, even the last pungent warning.

Our belief in your right to your form of government, and in the similar right of the American people and every other people, stems from our conviction that each individual has the right to choose his own destiny in freedom. This is the essence of our American heritage.

Our traditions go beyond the oceans which border our country. They have their origins in every country—Russia is certainly one—in which men of courage have challenged authoritarian institutions and have worked to win rights that could not be violated by their rulers. We had then and have today the good fortune to be a haven for men who were determined to remain free.

We have retained our links with the past without revolutionary disruption. But we have changed vastly. We are changing now. We must change—since progress creates new situations and our society is far from perfect.

If the American system is described simply as "Capitalism," its whole essence is missed. We hold to the freedom of an individual to apply his talents and means of fulfilling the needs of his community and to profit from this effort, if he can meet his neighbors' needs better or more cheaply than his competitor. At the same time we engage in voluntary co-operatives, especially in the fields of agricultural sales, housing, medicine, and social works. We assign Government an economic role—when Government can do for the people what they themselves cannot do so well or do at all.

Choosing what works best in each situation is characteristic of Americans. They will study and test any worthy proposal; continuously try new ways and change old patterns in a most worthy purpose to assure the pursuit of happiness by the individual in freedom and dignity under a framework of law legislated by freely elected representatives responsive to the will of the majority.

The system which provides us with the best opportunity to work toward the realization of our ideals may not suit you. That is for you to decide. Yours does not suit us. We do not believe that our system any more than yours is the inevitable solution for the other peoples of the world. They must, as we are doing, seek their own way, taking what they wish from the experience of others.

Our concern is that it be genuinely their way; that it be the product of their choice, of their heritage, and of their growth, not of interference by other powers.

We work for a world in which this diverse development will be guaranteed. We do not seek a world divided into co-existing camps locked in a struggle for supremacy. We hope for and work for a single world community which recognizes and respects a code of international law governing the relations between diverse peoples.

Briefly, plainly, candidly, I have tried to tell you of the American system and purpose as I see them. So complex a way of life, so varied in its expressions, comprising the lives of so many millions of people and so many ventures in human affairs cannot be compressed into a talk of fifteen minutes—or fifteen hours, for that matter. But I hope that I may have aroused in you an interest to learn more about us, more often to look through this "Window on the West" to America where, even as here, a just and enduring peace among all nations is the great human goal.

If you give me that response, I shall be in your debt all my life.

PEACE WITH JUSTICE

ADDRESS AT THE FIFTEENTH

GENERAL ASSEMBLY OF THE UNITED NATIONS

SEPTEMBER 22, 1960

The people of the United States join me in saluting those countries which, at this session of the General Assembly, are to be represented for the first time. With the admission of new members, mainly from the giant continent of Africa, almost one hundred nations will be joined in a common effort to construct permanent peace, with justice, in a sorely troubled world.

The drive of self-determination and of rising human aspirations is creating a new world of independent nations of Africa, even as it is producing a new world of both ferment and of promise in all developing areas. An awakening humanity in these regions demands as never before that we make a renewed attack on poverty, illiteracy, and disease.

Side by side with these startling changes, technology is also in revolution. It has brought forth terrifying weapons of destruction, which for the future of civilization, must be brought under control through a workable system of disarmament. And it has also opened up a new world of outer space, a celestial world filled with both bewildering problems and dazzling promise.

This is, indeed, a moment for honest appraisal and historic decision.

PRESIDENT EISENHOWER ADDRESSES THE FIFTEENTH GENERAL ASSEMBLY

OF THE UNITED NATIONS, SEPTEMBER, 1960

We can strive to master these problems for narrow national advantage or we can begin at once to undertake a period of constructive action which will subordinate selfish interest to the general well-being of the international community.

The choice is truly a momentous one.

Today, I come before you because our human commonwealth is once again in a state of anxiety and turmoil. Urgent issues confront us.

II

The first proposition I place before you is that only through the United Nations Organization can humanity make real and universal progress toward the goal of peace with justice. I believe that to support the United Nations Organization and its properly constituted mechanisms and selected officers is the road of greatest promise in peaceful progress. To attempt to hinder or stultify the United Nations or to deprecate its importance is to contribute to world unrest and, indeed, to incite the crises that from time to time so disturb all men. The United States stands squarely and unequivocally in support of the United Nations and those acting under its mandate in the interest of peace.

Nowhere is the challenge to the international community and to peace and orderly progress more evident than in Africa, rich in human and natural resources and bright with promise. Recent events there have brought into being what is, in effect, a vast continent of newly independent nations.

Outside interference with these newly emerging nations, all eager to undertake the tasks of modernization, has created a serious challenge to the authority of the United Nations.

That authority has grown steadily during the fifteen years since the United Nations pledged, in the words of its Charter, "to bring about by peaceful means, and in conformity with the principles of justice and international law, adjustments or settlement of international disputes or situations which might lead to a breach of the peace."

During those years, the United Nations successfully supported Iran's efforts to obtain the withdrawal of foreign military forces; played a significant role in preserving the independence of Greece, rallied World resistance to aggression against the Republic of Korea; helped to settle the Suez crisis; countered the threat to Lebanon's integrity; and most recently, has taken on an even more important task.

In response to the call of the Republic of the Congo, the United Nations, under its outstanding Secretary General, has recently mounted a large-scale effort to provide that new Republic with help. That effort has been flagrantly attacked by a few nations which wish to prolong strife in the Congo for their own selfish purposes. The criticism directed by these nations against the Secretary General, who has honorably and effectively fulfilled the mandate which he received from the United Nations, is nothing less than a direct attack upon the United Nations itself. He has earned the support of every peace loving nation.

The people of the Congo are entitled to build up their country in peace and freedom. Intervention by other nations in their internal affairs would deny them that right and create a focus of conflict in the heart of Africa.

The issue thus posed in the Congo could well arise elsewhere in Africa.

The resolution of this issue will determine whether the

United Nations is able to protect not only the new nations of Africa, but also other countries against outside pressures. It is the smaller nations that have the greatest stake in the effective functioning of the United Nations.

If the United Nations system is successfully subverted in Africa, the world will be on its way back to the traditional exercise of power politics in which small countries will be used as pawns by aggressive major powers. Any nation, seduced by glittering promises into becoming a catspaw for an imperialistic power, thereby undermines the United Nations and places in jeopardy the independence of itself and all others.

It is imperative that the international community protect the newly emerging nations of Africa from outside pressures that threaten their independence and their sovereign rights.

To this end, I propose a program which contains five major elements:

First: A pledge by all countries represented at this Assembly to respect the African peoples' right to choose their own way of life and to determine for themselves the course they wish to follow. This pledge would involve these specific commitments:

To refrain from intervening in these new nations' internal affairs by subversion, force, propaganda, or any other means.

To refrain from generating disputes beween the states of this area or from encouraging them to wasteful and dangerous competition in armaments.

And to refrain from any action to intensify or exploit present unsettled conditions in the Congo; by sending arms or forces into that troubled area; or by inciting its leaders and peoples to violence against each other.

These actions my country, and many others, are now avoiding. I hope this Assembly will call upon all its members to do likewise, and that each speaker who follows me to this platform will solemnly pledge his country to honor this call.

Second: The United Nations should be prepared to help the African countries maintain their security without wasteful and dangerous competition in armaments.

United Nations experts are being asked to train the Congo's security forces. If the Secretary General should find it useful to undertake increased activity in order to meet requests of this nature elsewhere, my country would be glad to join other Member States in making essential contributions to such United Nations activity.

More importantly I hope that the African states will use existing or establish new regional machinery in order to avert an arms race in this area. In so doing, they would help to spare their continent the ravages which the excesses of chauvinism have inflicted in the past. If, through concerted effort, these nations can choke off competition in armaments, they can give the whole world a welcome lesson in international relations.

The outstanding speed and success of the United Nations in dispatching substantial forces to the Congo should give these states assurance that they can rely on the United Nations to organize an effective response if their security is threatened. This should reduce any pressures on them to raise larger forces than are required to maintain internal security. Thus they would help to free their resources for more constructive purposes.

Third: We should all support the United Nations response

to emergency needs in the Republic of the Congo which the Secretary General has shown such skill in organizing. I hope that states represented here will pledge substantial resources to this international program, and agree that it should be the preferred means of meeting the Congo's emergency needs. The United States supports the establishment of a United Nations fund for the Congo. We are prepared to join other countries by contributing substantially for immediate emergency needs to the $100 million program that the Secretary General is proposing.

Fourth: The United Nations should help newly developing African countries to shape their long-term modernization programs. To this end:

The United Nations Special Fund and Expanded Technical Assistance Program should be increased so that in combination they can reach their annual $100 million goal in 1961. The Special Fund's functions should be expanded so that it can assist countries in planning economic development.

The United Nations Operational and Executive Personnel program for making available trained administrators to newly developing countries should be expanded and placed on a permanent basis. The United States is prepared to join other countries in contributing increased funds for this program, for the Special Fund, and for the United Nations Technical Assistance Program.

The World Bank and International Monetary Fund should be encouraged increasingly to provide counsel to the developing countries of Africa through missions and resident advisers. We should also look forward to appropriate and timely financial assistance from these two multilateral financial sources as the emerging countries qualify for their aid.

Of course, many forms of aid will be needed: both public and private on a bilateral and multilateral basis. For this assistance to be most effective it must be related to the basic problems and changing needs of the African countries themselves.

Fifth: As the final element of this program, I propose an all-out United Nations effort to help African countries launch such educational activities as they may wish to undertake.

It is not enough that loud-speakers in the public square exhort people to freedom. It is also essential that the people should be furnished with the mental tools to preserve and develop their freedom.

The United States is ready to contribute to an expanded program of educational assistance to Africa by the family of United Nations organizations, carried out as the Secretary General may deem appropriate, and according to the requests of the African nations themselves.

One of the first purposes of this assistance, after consultation with and approval by the governments involved, might be to establish, staff, and maintain—until these governments or private agencies could take over—Institutes for Health Education, for Vocational Training, for Public Administration and Statistics, and perhaps other purposes.

Each institute would be appropriately located and specifically dedicated to training the young men and women of that vast region, who are now called upon to assume the incredibly complex and important responsibilities inherent in an explosive emergence into nationhood.

If the African States should wish to send large numbers of their citizens for training abroad under this program, my country would be glad to set up a special commission to cooperate with the United Nations in arranging to accommodate many more of these students in our institutions of learning.

These then are the five ingredients of the Program I propose for Africa:

Noninterference in the African countries' internal affairs;

Help in assuring their security without wasteful and dangerous competition in armaments;

Emergency aid to the Congo;

International assistance in shaping long-term African development programs;

United Nations aid for education.

III

Such a program could go far to assure the African countries the clear chance at the freedom, domestic tranquility and progress they deserve.

The changes which are occurring in Africa are also evident elsewhere. Indeed, Africa is but one part of the new world of change and progress which is emerging in all the developing areas.

We must carry forward and intensify our programs of assistance for the economic and social development in freedom of other areas, particularly in Latin America, Asia, and the Middle East.

Beyond this, we must never forget that there are hundreds of millions of people, particularly in the less developed parts of the world, suffering from hunger and malnutrition, even though a number of countries, my own included, are producing food in surplus. This paradox should not continue.

The United States is already carrying out substantial programs to make its surpluses available to countries of greatest need. My country is also ready to join with other members of the United Nations in devising a workable scheme to provide food to member states through the United Nations system, relying on the advice and assistance of the Food and Agriculture Organization.

I hope this Assembly will seriously consider a specific program for carrying forward the promising Food for Peace Program.

IV

In the developing areas, we must seek to promote peaceful change, as well as to assist economic and social progress. To do this, to assist peaceful change, the international community must be able to manifest its presence in emergencies through United Nations observers or forces.

I should like to see member countries take positive action on the suggestions in the Secretary General's report looking to the creation of a qualified staff within the Secretariat to assist him in meeting future needs for United Nations forces.

To regularize the United Nations emergency force potential, I proposed in 1958 creation of stand-by arrangements for United Nations forces. Some progress has been made since then. Much remains to be done.

The Secretary General has now suggested that members should maintain a readiness to meet possible future requests from the United Nations for contributions to such forces.

All countries represented here should respond to this need, by earmarking national contingents which could take part in United Nations forces in case of need.

The time to do it is now—at this Assembly.

I assure countries which now receive assistance from the United States that we favor use of that assistance to help them maintain such contingents in the state of readiness suggested by the Secretary General. To assist the Secretary General's efforts, the United States is prepared to earmark substantial air and sea transport facilities on a stand-by basis, to help move contingents requested by the United Nations in any future emergency.

Over the long run, further progress toward increasing the United Nations' ability to respond to future needs is surely possible. The prospects for such progress, however, will remain just that—prospects—unless we move now to exploit the immediate possibilities for practical action suggested by the Secretary General.

V

Another problem confronting us involves outer space.

The emergency of this new world poses a vital issue: Will outer space be preserved for peaceful use and developed for the benefit of all mankind? Or will it become another focus for the arms race, and thus an area of dangerous and sterile competition?

The choice is urgent. It is ours to make.

The nations of the world have recently united in declaring the continent of Antarctica "off limits" to the military preparations. We could extend this principle to an even more important sphere. National vested interests have not yet been developed in space or in celestial bodies. Barriers to agreement are now lower than they will ever be again.

The opportunity may be fleeting. Before many years have passed, the point of no return may be behind us.

Let us remind ourselves that we had a chance in 1946 to ensure that atomic energy be devoted exclusively to peaceful purposes. That chance was missed when the Soviet Union turned down the comprehensive plan submitted by the United States for placing atomic energy under international control.

We must not lose the chance we still have to control the future of outer space.

I propose that:

First: We agree that celestial bodies are not subject to national appropriation by any claims of sovereignty.

Second: We agree that the nations of the world shall not engage in warlike activities on these bodies.

Third: We agree, subject to appropriate verification, that no nation will put into orbit or station in outer space weapons of mass destruction. All launchings of space craft should be verified in advance by the United Nations.

Fourth: We press forward with a program of international co-operation for constructive peaceful uses of outer space under the United Nations. Better weather forecasting, improved world-wide communications, and more effective exploration not only of outer space but of our own earth; these are but a few of the benefits of such co-operation.

Agreement on these proposals would enable future generations to find peaceful and scientific progress, not another fearful dimension to the arms race, as they explore the universe.

VI

But armaments must also be controlled here on earth, if civilization is to be assured of survival. These efforts must extend both to conventional and nonconventional armaments.

My country has made specific proposals to this end during the past year. New United States proposals were put forward on June 27, with the hope that they could serve as the basis for negotiations to achieve general disarmament. The United States still supports these proposals.

The communist nations' walk-out at Geneva, when they learned that we were about to submit these proposals, brought negotiations to an abrupt halt. Their unexplained action does not, however, reduce the urgent need for arms control.

My country believes that negotiations can—and should—soon be resumed.

Our aim is to reach agreement on all the various measures that will bring general and complete disarmament. Any honest appraisal, however, must recognize that this is an immense task. It will take time.

We should not have to wait until we have agreed on all the detailed measures to reach this goal before we begin to move toward disarmament. Specific and promising steps to this end were suggested in our June 27 proposals.

If negotiations can be resumed, it may be possible to deal particularly with two pressing dangers—that of war by miscalculation and that of mounting nuclear weapons stock-piles.

The advent of missiles, with ever shorter reaction times, makes measures to curtail the danger of war by miscalculation increasingly necessary. States must be able quickly to assure each other that they are not preparing aggressive moves, particularly in international crises, when each side takes steps to improve its own defenses which might be misinterpreted by the other. Such misinterpretation in the absence of machinery to verify that neither was preparing to attack the other, could lead to a war which no one had intended.

Today the danger of war by miscalculation could be reduced, in times of crisis, by the intervention, when requested by any nation seeking to prove its own peaceful intention, of an appropriate United Nations surveillance body. The question of methods can be left to the experts.

Thus the vital issue is not a matter of technical feasibility but the political willingness of individual countries to submit to inspection. The United States has taken the lead in this field.

Today, I solemnly declare, on behalf of the United States, that we are prepared to submit to any international inspection, provided only that it is effective and truly reciprocal. This step we will take willingly as an earnest of our determination to uphold the preamble of the United Nations Charter, "to save succeeding generations from the scourge of war, which twice in our lifetime has brought untold sorrow to mankind. . . ."

The United States wants the Soviet Union and all the nations of the world to know enough about United States defense preparations to be assured that United States forces exist only for deterrence and defense—not for surprise attack. I hope the Soviet Union will similarly wish to assure the United States and other nations of the nonaggressive character of its security preparations.

There is a more basic point: In an age of rapidly developing technology, secrecy is not only an anachronism—it is downright dangerous. To seek to maintain a society in which a military move can be taken in complete secrecy, while professing a desire to reduce the risk of war through arms control, is a contradiction.

A second danger which ought to be dealt with in early negotiations is posed by the growth and prospective spread of nuclear weapons stockpiles.

To reverse this trend, I propose that the nations producing nuclear weapons immediately convene experts to design a system for terminating, under verification procedures, all production of fissionable materials for weapons purposes.

That termination would take effect as soon as the agreed inspection system has been installed and is operating effectively, while progress in other disarmament fields is also being sought.

The United States is prepared, in the event of a termination of production, to join the USSR in transferring substantial quantities of fissionable materials to international stockpiles. The United Nations Disarmament Commission has already heard the proposal of Ambassador Lodge, to set aside not pounds, as was proposed by the United States in 1954, but tons of fissionable materials for peaceful purposes. Additional transfers would be made as progress in other aspects of disarmament is accomplished.

If the USSR will agree to a cessation of production of fissionable materials for weapons purposes, some production facilities could be closed without delay. The United States would be willing to match the USSR in shutting down major plants producing fissionable materials, one by one, under international inspection and verification.

The proposed working group of experts could also consider how to verify the complete elimination of nuclear weapons, which is part of the third stage of our proposed disarmament program. There is as yet no known means of demonstrably accomplishing this; we would hope that the experts could develop a system.

United States officials are willing to meet immediately with representatives of other countries for a preliminary exchange of views on these proposals.

Some who have followed closely the many fruitless disarmament talks since the war tend to become cynical, to assume that the task is hopeless. This is not the position of the United States.

Men everywhere want to disarm. They want their wealth and labor to be spent not for war, but for food, for clothing, for shelter, for medicines, for schools.

Time and time again, the American people have voiced this yearning—to join with men of good will everywhere in building a better world. We always stand ready to consider any feasible proposal to this end. We ask only this: that such a program not give military advantage to any nation and that it permit men to inspect the disarmament of other nations.

A disarmament program which was not inspected and guaranteed would increase, not reduce, the risk of war.

The international control of atomic energy and general and complete disarmament can no more be accomplished by rhetoric than can the economic development of newly independent countries. Both of these immense tasks facing mankind call for serious, painstaking, costly, laborious and nonpropaganda approaches.

VII

I have specifically avoided in this address mention of several immediate problems that are troubling the United States and other nations. My failure to do so does not mean in any sense that they are not of great concern both to the United States and to the entire international community.

For example, accumulating evidence of threatening encroachments to the freedom of the people of West Berlin continues to disturb us deeply.

Though of special concern to the United States, the shooting down of an American aircraft last July first over international waters, the apparent killing of four of its crew members and the imprisonment of two others on trumped-up spy charges is a shocking affront to the right of all nations to peaceful passage on and over the high seas. By its veto in the Security Council the Soviet Union prevented a full investigation of the facts of the case. These facts still demand to be heard as a proper matter for the consideration of an impartial tribunal.

The particular problems I have just mentioned are not merely isolated instances of disagreements among a few nations. They are central to the issue of peace itself, and illustrative of the continuous and interdependent nature of our respective national concerns. They must be confronted with the earnestness and seriousness which their settlement demands.

VIII

The basic fact today of all change in the domain of international affairs is the need to forge the bonds and build the structure of a true world community.

The United Nations is available to mankind to help it create just such a community. It has accomplished what no nation singly, or any limited group of nations, could have accomplished. It has become the forum of all peoples, and the structure about which they can center their joint endeavors to create a better future for our world.

We must guard jealously against those who in alternating moods look upon the United Nations as an instrument for use or abuse. The United Nations was not conceived as an Olympian organ to amplify the propaganda tunes of individual nations.

The generating force behind a successful United Nations must be the noble idea that a true international community can build a peace with justice if only people will work together patiently in an atmosphere of open trust.

In urging progress toward a world community, I cite the American concept of the destiny of a progressive society. Here in what was once a wilderness we have generated a society and a civilization drawn from many sources. Yet out of this mixture of many peoples and faiths we have developed unity in freedom—a unity designed to protect the rights of each individual while enhancing the freedom and well-being of all.

This concept of unity in freedom, drawn from the diver-

sity of many racial strains and cultures, we would see made
a reality for all mankind. Opposed to the idea of two hostile,
embittered worlds in perpetual conflict, we envisage a single
world community, as yet unrealized but advancing steadily
toward fulfillment through our plans, our efforts, and our
collective acts.

Thus we see as our goal, not a super-state above nations,
but a world community embracing them all, rooted in law
and justice and enhancing the potentialities and common
purposes of all peoples.

As we enter the decade of the 1960's, let us launch a renewed effort to strengthen this international community;
to forge new bonds between its members in undertaking
new ventures on behalf of all mankind.

As we take up this task, let us not delude ourselves that
the absence of war alone is a sufficient basis for a peaceful
world. I repeat, we must also build a world of justice under
law, and we must overcome poverty, illiteracy, and disease.

We of the United States will join with you in making a
mounting effort to build the structure of true peace—a peace
in which all peoples may progress constantly to higher levels
of human achievement. The means are at hand. We have but
to use them with a wisdom and energy worthy of our cause.

I commend this great task to your hearts, and minds, and
willing hands. Let us go forward together, leaving none behind.